T0368150

# POWER ⬆UP

## 7 TRANSFORMATIONAL STEPS
### TO OWN YOUR POWER AND HAVE
### MORE JOY IN YOUR LIFE!

JACKIE CAWLEY, DO, MBA

**BALBOA.**PRESS
A DIVISION OF HAY HOUSE

Balboa Press books may be ordered through booksellers or by contacting:

Balboa Press
A Division of Hay House
1663 Liberty Drive
Bloomington, IN 47403
www.balboapress.com
844-682-1282

Because of the dynamic nature of the Internet, any web addresses or links contained in this book may have changed since publication and may no longer be valid. The views expressed in this work are solely those of the author and do not necessarily reflect the views of the publisher, and the publisher hereby disclaims any responsibility for them.

The author of this book does not dispense medical advice or prescribe the use of any technique as a form of treatment for physical, emotional, or medical problems without the advice of a physician, either directly or indirectly. The intent of the author is only to offer information of a general nature to help you in your quest for emotional and spiritual well-being. In the event you use any of the information in this book for yourself, which is your constitutional right, the author and the publisher assume no responsibility for your actions.

Any people depicted in stock imagery provided by Getty Images are models, and such images are being used for illustrative purposes only. Certain stock imagery © Getty Images.

Print information available on the last page.

ISBN: 979-8-7652-5640-4 (sc)
ISBN: 979-8-7652-5639-8 (e)

Library of Congress Control Number: 2024921626

Balboa Press rev. date: 12/13/2024

For Katie and CJ, who have been my greatest teachers, and for my husband and best friend.

# CONTENTS

# PREFACE

I have always had a love of reading and writing and have wanted to write a book for several years. I did not actually believe I could be a published author, until I rediscovered myself, and found my voice. Through a series of unexpected life events, I was suddenly provided with the time and space I needed to reflect on my career and personal life. I also had the chance to meet a literary agent who taught me about the publishing world. She showed me how to write a book proposal and gave me constructive feedback on my writing and ideas. We met by chance, and instantly connected. She even called me her "soul sister." Looking back, I know that it was not just a chance meeting but synchronicity at work. Events began to unfold, and I had the opportunity to write, create and complete this book.

This is the book that I could have used much earlier in my career. Before I lost a bit of my authentic self as I moved up the corporate healthcare ladder. As a physician executive I was respected for my leadership skills, and I was very productive, effective, and successful. I was rewarded for my hard work with promotions and became the first woman to be medical staff president at the largest hospital in the state of Maine. I had a wonderful husband; a lovely home and we raised two amazing children. To others, I had it all, a distinguished career and wonderful personal life. Inside I suffered from imposter syndrome and lacked self-confidence. I tried to work within a power structure that never seemed to be a "fit." I lost my voice and at times gave my power to others, such as my boss or the most senior executive officer of the organization. I was frustrated, felt stuck, and underappreciated for my contributions. I also felt less joy in my life. When I was gifted the chance to step away from work, I made the choice to learn and grow as much as I could spiritually, emotionally, and mentally. I focused on healing my body, mind, and spirit.

During that break I applied all that I had coached and taught to others to myself and developed a framework for transformative personal growth. I became empowered to start my own business and change my professional path. I found my voice and began to write. I realized more daily joy and happiness as I focused on my own healing, self-care, and self-compassion. The outcome has been more than I could have hoped for. I have been able to apply the concepts and content in this framework with myself, and to my clients, and have seen them transform and grow. My clients have become more energized, happier and empowered to push out of their comfort zones and challenge themselves personally and professionally. It has been so rewarding to see their growth and be able to be of service to them. My purpose has always been to help others heal and thrive.

I wrote this book with the goal of helping others to learn to find their voice and their joy. To be more empowered, to live as their authentic selves and shine their light with the world. To know that they have infinite capacity and possibility to live the future they envision for themselves. As a doctor I had the gift of being present with the people I served. With a book, I hope to connect with others as if you were in my office or clinic. To be able to help you heal and grow. I am honored that you chose this book to read and hope that you find it both informative and transformative. My truest wish is that it will serve you and help you reach your highest potential and best authentic self.

Love and Light,
Jackie

# MY STORY

I have been an osteopathic family physician for thirty years, and in leadership roles for most of that time. I have had the privilege to care for thousands of patients and to develop and lead innovative programs to support health care transformation. This work has included teaching and coaching other physicians and members of my health care teams in leadership and personal development. All my career, I focused on improving patient care outcomes, the quality and processes of care delivery and care team satisfaction. It has been quite a career, and I am proud of what I have accomplished and learned along the way. I also must admit I needed a lot of development myself. Looking back at my younger self, I laugh and shake my head as I recall some of my actions and behaviors. Some were so positive, like standing in front of my team members and sharing my vision for the future. Seeing their excitement and reactions. I would walk away from those encounters energized and humbled by their response. I was able to inspire and motivate them. That surprised me.

A nurse told me that I had made a difference in her life, as she moved forward to pursue a nursing master's degree. A patient of mine told me I was their "angel," simply because I was present with them as they healed from severe trauma. I was not self-aware enough at the time to understand the impact I could have on others. On the flip side, I also recall being in meetings where I believed if I was loud and forceful enough, I could get others to buy into my ideas or plans for improvement. Again, I did not have the self-awareness to know when to adjust my behaviors or how to best manage them and the emotions of others to get the results I desired.

Over the years I read leadership development books, self-development books and sought coaches and mentors to help me grow as a person and a leader. I then began to compile these learnings and develop leadership development programs for others. Leadership like life is a journey, and there is never a true destination. I was honored to help support others on their journeys as a coach, teacher, or mentor. My whole career I was able to be the three things I had always wanted to be: a healer, teacher, and leader.

It is a miracle I made it to being a physician. I grew up in a dysfunctional family. My parents married as teenagers and my mother suffered from mental illness and was addicted to alcohol and pain medications. Our home life was chaotic and even traumatic at times. I look back at my childhood and feel that it was a good one. Despite the drama and emotional and physical neglect my brother, sister and I endured. As the oldest I had to grow up very quickly as a "mother" to my mother, and to look after my siblings. Luckily, we had a strong family network of loving adults who were always there to support and care for us.

As a child, I loved reading, writing and being outdoors. I knew from an early age that I was going to be a doctor. It was a calling for me, and I wanted to help others. My father was the first in our entire family to get a college degree, so to believe that I could become a doctor was a bit of a stretch. We did not have the money to pay for college, much less a medical school education. However, that didn't stop me. I think it only fueled me to prove to myself and my family that I could do it on my own and become the doctor I was meant to be. I left home to go to college and enjoyed my independence. In my third year of college. I learned about osteopathic medicine and decided that was what I wanted to be. An osteopathic physician, with a philosophy, that had the mind, body and spirit all connected. A philosophy grounded in the belief that the body had the ability to heal itself, and that a hands-on treatment of patients supported that healing. It fit with my values, passions and purpose. I think I knew my authentic self-better at that time than I did as a "mature" adult in my forties, with a lot of life experience.

I was thrilled to be accepted to medical school in Maine and met my husband on the third day of school. He was in the class ahead of me and we met at a party and talked for hours. It was as if we had always known one another. Two years later we married and have been together ever since. We have built a wonderful life together and raised our two children. They are caring and accomplished adults. It was not always easy, and we had our tough times. The journey was worth it. I had carried a lot of my scars from my childhood into adulthood with me. I tended to be a perfectionist, a people pleaser, and made sure others were cared for first, rather than myself. I lacked self-confidence and at times suffered from imposter syndrome. I had a fear that I would not be accepted for my "real" self. I had a few bouts of depression and drank a lot more wine than I should have. I was also a workaholic and spent more hours working than then is healthy. I was always trying to prove that I was worthy of being a senior executive leader. The result was a lack of proper self-care and time to recharge my own batteries. I was on the verge of burnout several times along the way. The last time was the hardest. It was a result of working through the COVID pandemic full-time while also dealing with health issues myself and in my immediate family. I was mentally and emotionally exhausted, and physically affected. It was a tough couple of years, but I adopted a growth mindset and tried my best to be open to what life was guiding me towards. Life was an excellent teacher for me. It pushed me to rediscover myself and what was profoundly important to me.

Our family was able to navigate through our health issues, and then the unexpected happened. In the middle of the night, as I headed to the bathroom, I had a syncopal episode – I fainted without warning. The fall resulted in a gash to my head, and broken bones in my neck in several places. I had to be rushed to the state trauma center and have two surgeries to repair the damage to my cervical spine. I spent five days in the hospital unable to stand or even sit up without help. My blood pressure kept dropping dangerously low. It was painful and traumatic for myself and my family, especially after we had been through so much the previous few years. I knew that it could have been much worse. I knew that I could have been paralyzed or even killed by the fall. It was a sobering discovery.

The recovery period gave me time to reflect on my life. Which was sobering too. I was able to acknowledge and celebrate my many accomplishments and all that I had learned, but I also had to acknowledge and accept where I had strayed from what was most important to me. The long recovery time was a gift. It allowed me to dig deep and question what I wanted for myself and my family moving forward. It gave me the chance to accept and love myself. It helped me to see where I had committed self-sabotage and invented my own internal glass ceiling. I had to take accountability for my life.

I learned to care for myself better by reestablishing my spiritual daily practices, and focusing on healing physically, emotionally, and spiritually. I found my voice and decided it was time to use it. Oddly enough, I prayed that I would be let go at work, so that I could spend time on what I really wanted to do. To write, start a new business, and help others find their way back to themselves. Within two months of returning to work, my boss called me into her office and told me she had eliminated my position. Once the shock to my ego wore off, I was elated. I was able to take an early retirement. I had the time to take all that I had learned and share it with others. I had time to focus on my own self-care journey and healing. I had time to spend with the people whom I loved. I had the time to rediscover me. I know that I have more work to do to on my self-healing journey. I know that I have so much more to learn. I am grateful for all the life experiences that have brought me to this place and time. I wouldn't change a thing.

# INTRODUCTION

# How To Use This Book

Welcome to the POWER UP framework for transformational personal development. This book will provide you with a step-by-step process to help you on your journey to your best self.

The book is divided into three sections, each focused on specific topic areas that comprise the POWER UP model for transformation. Every chapter reviews a step in the POWER UP framework and includes a set of prompts to reflect upon and use in journaling. At the end of each chapter is a set of POWER POINTS that summarize the key themes and highlights of the chapter. Journaling and self-reflection are a crucial part of this transformation process and so make sure to have paper, a journal, or your favorite device easily accessible to capture your thoughts, feelings and learning as you move through the book.

The POWER UP framework for transformation includes seven steps to guide the reader in their personal development journey. Each chapter focuses on a single step in the process. Why is the book titled POWER UP? POWER UP is a mnemonic to help you remember the steps in the framework. It is an acronym and includes the following steps.

Pause, and rediscover you
Observe, and reflect on your choices and current state

Wonder, discover how you got here
Expose, be conscious of your limiting beliefs
Replace, you have the power to reframe
Unlock, reveal your highest potential
Possibility, embrace a possibility mindset

### Figure 1: POWER UP Framework

## POWER UP FRAMEWORK

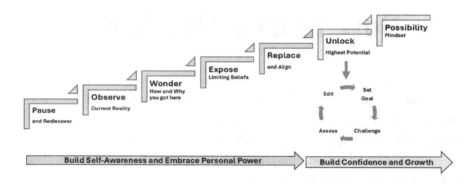

The book is divided into three sections, to allow the reader to move through the steps of the framework and learn its key concepts in a more organized and intuitive way. The first section is "Getting to Know You." It is centered on helping you to build and strengthen your level of self-awareness. It will provide exercises and prompts to help you better understand what is most important to you and to develop a vision statement for yourself for the future. It also includes a chapter that will ask you to compare where you are in your current life to what you most desire for yourself in the future. Section Two is titled Power Play. It is focused on exposing your limiting beliefs and outdated narratives that you have developed over time and replacing them with a new way of thinking and experiencing yourself and the world. It will help you to become more empowered and understand where and when you have given your power to others. It will also compare masculine and feminine power models and provide you with an understanding of which model you most resonate with. The final Section, Rise and Shine, will provide you with tools to help to push yourself out of your comfort zone and into learning and growth zones using small cycles of challenges to build self-confidence and resilience. It will encourage you to adopt a possibility mindset and reach for your highest potential.

You have the choice to follow the book section by section, or to focus on specific chapters based on your individual personal development needs and interests. There is no right way to use this book, just as there is no "right" way to develop and transform. The choice is yours and should be centered on what you feel is best suited for you, or that resonates with you at this point in your journey. I hope that you enjoy this book as much as I have enjoyed writing it and wish you much success on your transformation journey.

# SECTION I
# GETTING TO KNOW YOU

*"Let go of who you think you should be in order to be who you are"*
*Brene Brown*

# CHAPTER 1

# PAUSE

## Take time to reflect and rediscover who you are

*"Without reflection we go blindly on our way."*
Margaret J. Wheatley

HAVE YOU EVER LOOKED AT YOURSELF IN THE MIRROR AND ASKED "why am I doing this? Or "How did I get here?" Do you feel as if somehow you have strayed from what you had originally planned for yourself? Perhaps compromised yourself in some way to be accepted, get the promotion, or make things okay for someone else in your life? It would not be unusual.

We all must make choices as we move through our life journey. And some of them can pull us off the path we had hoped to follow or push aside a dream we had for ourselves. Family obligations, financial strains, medical illness of a partner or other such life twists and turns can pull us off our course. Reflection and taking time to build or strengthen your self-awareness can help you get back on track. However, you need to be very intentional and willing to do the work.

In my leadership development work with other physicians, I used an approach with them to help them define their core values and professional vision for the future. Then, I would have them use this

JACKIE CAWLEY, DO, MBA

information to write a professional mission and vision statement. This would allow them to be more focused on what they needed to further develop their leadership skills and give them more clarity when making career choices for themselves. We would not do this work in the middle of a busy day at the hospital or clinic. Instead, we would spend several hours in a more relaxed setting so that they could have the luxury of time to reflect and discuss their ideas and vision for themselves. They could pause and take the time to be clear on what was most important to them professionally. The result would be a simple statement for them to use going forward. For example, my vision statement at that time was to help lead transformation in health care and help organize other physicians to do the same. That statement was what I bounced decisions against when making career choices for myself. I did a similar exercise for my personal life, and with my husband to apply to our family life and decision making.

Reflection and self-awareness are critical skills to have as a leader and manager. It is also incredibly helpful in making sure you are in alignment in your personal life. It is something that requires you to pause and take time to do the work. Ok, so you cannot just press pause in your life like you can with a Netflix movie or Apple tunes, but wouldn't that be nice? To have the chance to pause, ponder and clarify what is most important to you? You may not be able to press a button and take a vacation from life, but you can get to know yourself better. You can pause and rediscover who you are. How do I know this to be true? Because I have personally used this approach and reaped its benefits. I have used this approach with others and have witnessed firsthand its positive impacts. It is not a radical new approach. It is applying the basics of building self-awareness with a few added steps. It is called the Pause and Rediscover Process.

## The Pause and Rediscover Process:

The goal of this process is to help you define for yourself what your life purpose is and to create a vision statement for your future self. You cannot be successful in doing this until you spend time reflecting to better understand your core values, your passions and to list and describe your special superpowers. What are your special superpowers? The unique set of skills, talent, experience and knowledge that only you have. There is only one of you on this earth, and you have a purpose which is important and yours alone. You have limitless possibilities for your future. You just need to work through the process of discovering and defining that for yourself.

Developing a personal vision statement can be very empowering and provides you with a focus for your future best self! It will help you define your goals, dreams, and aspirations, and support you in your development journey, both personally and professionally. To get started, follow the series of exercises and prompts below to clarify your values, passions, unique skill sets and purpose. This will provide you with the information you need to create your vision statement.

### Figure 2: The Pause and Rediscover Process

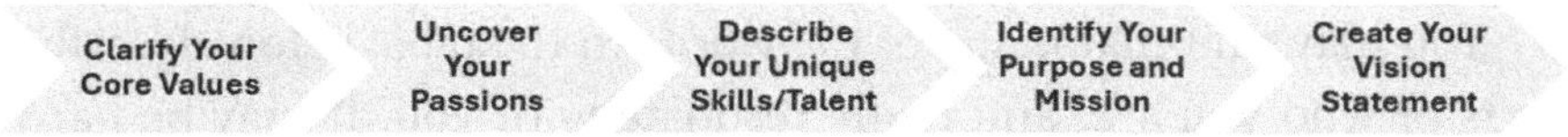

| Clarify Your Core Values | Uncover Your Passions | Describe Your Unique Skills/Talent | Identify Your Purpose and Mission | Create Your Vision Statement |
|---|---|---|---|---|

## Exercise 1: Clarify Your Core Values:

The first exercise is to identify your core values. For example, my core values include integrity, accountability, compassion, gratitude, and family. Values are the beliefs and standards by which we behave and act in our daily lives. They are the core principles by which we live and make decisions. We all have them, even if they have not been recognized or vocalized. We learn them from our family of origin, society and our cultural and religious communities. They become ingrained in us and influence our actions and behaviors. When we are confronted with a situation where there is a discrepancy between our values and the values of another, we feel it. We sense it. A feeling of angst or an uncomfortable sensation in our gut or chest. Something feels "not right," or "off."

Values may be ingrained, but they are not stagnant. Your values can evolve over time. What is important to you as a twenty-something may not be the same as when you have a partner, children, or position where you are responsible for a team of people or the safety of others. That is why it is helpful to periodically reflect on your values and what is most core and fundamental in how you want to live and work. It is helpful to do this exercise every few years or at times of major life transitions. For example, gratitude was not one of my original core values when I was twenty, but it has become one over the past several years as I have grown spiritually and emotionally.

How to identify and clarify your core values? Below is a table of common personal values adapted from James Clear and the LeaderShape Institute. Read the following values and check off the ones that most resonate with you at this time in your life. Pick as many as you would like to start with and write that list down. Next, review your list of values and narrow that initial list down to your top 3-5 values.

You may find that many of the words in the table below describe parts of who you are, and really resonate with you. It may be hard to pick the top 3-5 core values for yourself. The difference between the values that resonate with you and describe you vs. what is most core for you are your non-negotiables. In other words, if push came to shove you would hold your ground and not act or behave in a way that would conflict with those 3-5 most core, non-negotiable values. One way to uncover those most essential values is to think of a time when you felt angry or uncomfortable in a situation with another person, or where you felt compromised in some way. If you felt that way, it is likely that the other person was demonstrating a value that was in conflict with yours. The reason it felt wrong or "off" to you was because it clashed with one of your non-negotiable, most essential core values. This simple question can help you see what does not feel right, and what value is not yours. Usually the opposite action or behavior, the opposite value, is more "you." More consistent with how you think people should act or behave. That would make it one of your core values.

The list below is a summary of possible values. It is always okay to add to the list if there is something missing that you feel is of value to you.

**Table 1: Personal Values List:**

| Accountability | Beauty | Fairness | Health |
|---|---|---|---|
| Authenticity | Calmness | Faith | Integrity |
| Adventurous | Compassion | Fame | Independence |
| Achievement | Caring | Family | Influence |
| Autonomy | Challenge | Fun | Kindness |
| Altruism | Community | Freedom | Knowledge |
| Assertiveness | Creativity | Growth | Leadership |
| Ambition | Contentment | Grace | Learning |
| Balance | Contribution | Happiness | Love |
| Boldness | Determination | Honesty | Loyalty |
| Belonging | Excellence | Hard work | Meaningful Work |

| Make a Difference | Responsibility | Self-Reliance | Uniqueness |
|---|---|---|---|
| Optimism | Reliability | Strategic | Unity |
| Openness | Recognition | Strength | Understanding |
| Originality | Service | Teamwork | Wealth |
| Peace | Spirituality | Trustworthiness | Welcoming |
| Prosperity | Stability | Tolerance | Wisdom |
| Popularity | Success | Thankfulness | Witty |
| Respect | Status | Timeliness | Wonder |
| Other | Other | Other | Other |

Many of the values in the table above may resonate with you and how you want to live your life. Once you have narrowed the list down to the top 3-5 values, check to make sure they are ones that are non-negotiable for you and are your most core set of values.

Exercise 2: Uncover Your Passions:

Your passions are the things, ideas or activities you get excited about. They evoke strong feelings and powerful emotions in you. Your passions are what light you up inside. What makes your heart sing. I have been fortunate to have my passions be front in center in my work and life. That is not always true for everyone. The Merriam-Webster dictionary defines them as the activities, concepts or things we have a desire or strong liking, or even a devotion for. I think that is spot on, which is why they can evoke such powerful emotions. Do you have the chance to live or work doing the things that you are passionate about? If so, that is awesome. Not everyone has the luxury to be focused on what lights them up inside. They need to choose a job to make ends meet, put food on the table or adjust their life to attend to children or other family members. But even if you cannot make a living doing what you are passionate about, you can integrate them into your daily life.

It can be a bit overwhelming for you to describe them or list them, but as you do you continue to build self-awareness. One way to achieve this is to ask yourself how you would feel if you were living and acting on your passions? Would you feel joy and excitement? Would you feel exhilarated and energized? Perhaps you would feel centered and focused. Try to describe the emotions and the feelings fully, and then ask yourself if you have ever felt those same feelings in the past.

Think about that time and what you were doing, what you were thinking, and at what point in your life this was occurring. When you ask these questions and focus on your feelings and emotions it can bring about a type of "aha" moment for you. You may even laugh or smile at the thought of that moment or memory. It may suddenly feel so simple to identify and describe them. And it is. All you need to know is inside of you. You just need to take the time to ask and to listen to yourself. To listen to your inner wisdom and authentic self, not about what you are "supposed to do" but what lights you up and lifts your heart.

If you go back to your childhood or young adulthood, you will recall the things you most enjoyed doing. The activities that brought you joy and made you happy. These are often the root of your passions, you just forgot them or lacked time for them along the way as you grew into an adult. There may have also been things or ideas that you felt very strongly about or that you had conviction about. You felt them deeply. You felt them in your bones, your heart and your soul. When you were engaged in those activities time seemed to fly by and you felt in the flow, a state where it felt effortless and natural. For example, I loved to read, write, dance and be in nature as a child. I would spend hours sitting in an apple tree in our backyard reading. I would write short stories, poems and plays to put on for family and friends. As I grew into adulthood, I lacked time to write for enjoyment. My writing was centered on grant applications and white papers, or presentations to senior leaders. Reading was focused on learning the latest advances in medicine and health care administration, rather than for fun. I tried to fit in dance classes here and there, and my time in nature would be scheduled walks for 30 minutes whenever I could fit into my schedule. Not exactly living my passions, right?

My other passion was helping others, which I had the daily chance to do as a physician, and that was very gratifying. I loved working with patients and getting the satisfaction of caring for them and helping them in their healing. I lost that connection when I moved full time into health care administration. I still was helping others, just in a very disconnected way from the patient. Going through this exercise myself, I was able to rediscover my passion for writing and directly working with other people to support their healing and development. I also rediscovered my love of movement and combining it with nature through mindfulness practices such as yoga, meditative walking in nature and paddle boarding.

In using this technique with clients, I have seen them rediscover their love of crafting, arithmetic, cooking and art. All things they had dropped along the way due to competing priorities and family life. Watching them rediscover their passions and pick them back up has been so gratifying as I watched them have more joy in their daily life. Now it is time for you to rediscover yours.

To identify your passions ask yourself the questions below and record your answer.

- *What are you most passionate about?*
- *What are the things, activities, or ideas you have that get you really revved up and excited to work on or do?*
- *What are the things you like to do when you have spare time?*
- *What makes you feel happy and as if time seems to fly by for you?*
- *What brought you joy and made you happy as a child or young adult?*
- *What do you feel when you are doing something you are passionate about?*
- *What other time in your life did you have the same or similar feeling, as when doing something you are passionate about? What were you doing at that time?*

Living your passions motivates you and brings more fulfillment and joy to your life. It provides our life with more meaning. So much of the burnout we witness in the workplace is related to people not doing what makes their heart sing. Not working at something that is meaningful to them or that they love. Life is too short and unpredictable to just work to live and get by. You may not always be able to have a job that is in one of your areas of passion, but you can make the time in your life to pursue them. You can take them up as a hobby, volunteer for something you are passionate about, or try to find ways to incorporate them into your current job or set of responsibilities.

As an example, you may be inspired to work with other people and be of service. You may love cooking a new recipe for others, painting, teaching, or motivational speaking. If you consider your current job or set of responsibilities, you can figure out a way to combine a passion with what you do daily. Love to cook and work as a mechanic? Perhaps suggest a potluck lunch at work and bring in a special new recipe for your teammates to try. Maybe you are a stay-at-home parent with three kids under the age of five and love painting. How about hosting a neighborhood painting party to connect with other parents, provide the kids with playdate time and have the chance to bring out your inner artist. Your passion may be physical fitness and having your own fitness center or being a chief executive officer of an organization. The sky is the limit here, so you want to be sure to write down all the things you are enthusiastic and inspired about. You do not need to figure out right now how to fit them into your life, or when to act on them. You just need to identify them for yourself. As you move through the series of exercises, you will find a way to take these and incorporate them into your vision statement for yourself.

You may wonder why it was so easy to move away from the things that mattered so much to you in the past. As adults, we will often compromise our passions to get financial security, a promotion, a new title, or a stable family life. I had several exciting opportunities for new positions that were a perfect fit for my passions and experience. However, it required my family to move across the country and my husband, the primary breadwinner in our family, to find a new job. I had to compromise an awesome job that fit my passions for my family and stay in a role that was less fulfilling for me, but worked for my life at the time. I bet that something along those lines has happened for you as well, and for important reasons. We often compromise and do what we feel is the "right thing" or what we "should do" rather than go for what excites us and we are most motivated by. Over the years, I have learned that you can have both. A job or role that allows you to pursue your passions and stability at home or in other areas of your life. You can manifest what you most desire for your life if you are clear on what you want and believe it can be. You act is if it exists right now, in the present moment. The "how" and the timing may not be clear, but that is not important. What is important is being totally clear on identifying your passions and what you want from life, and then believing it can be true. Which brings us to the next step in the Pause and Rediscover Process, describing your skills and talents.

## Exercise 3: Describe Your Skills and Talents

In this exercise you will describe and document the skills, talents, knowledge and experiences that make you the unique individual that you are. No one else on the planet has your skillset, ideas, and unique way of seeing and experiencing the world. You have gifts that need to be shared with others. These are your special superpowers. You also need to take the time to recognize and celebrate all that you have learned and accomplished on your journey. To give yourself credit for all that you have achieved so far in this life. Take the time to document all your skills and talents, and not just the ones you think "matter" to your boss, parents, partner, or friends. For example, you excel at tinkering with small engines or cars. Write it down. Have a talent for interior decorating, painting, and project management? Write it down. Able to facilitate large groups to come to consensus as well as ability to cook like a master chef on the weekend? Jot it down. Collect and pay homage to all that you are and all that makes you uniquely you.

How does that feel? It can feel a little odd at first. We are not taught to hold ourselves in high esteem. To pat ourselves on the back or give recognition to ourselves. That would be bragging, showing off, or boasting, right? Who are you to hold yourself up high and give such credit to yourself? That is seen as obscene in our society, with its' collective mindset of scarcity. Where there are winners and losers. Where there is not enough success or resources available to all, and common, useful things may not be held in high regard. I would counter, why not you? We all have skills and talents and special gifts to share with the world. Every one of us. Approaching the world with a mindset of abundance, we understand that there are unlimited resources. There are infinite possibilities and the ability to achieve win-win solutions. With a mindset of abundance there is more than enough success to go around. Everyone has something to offer the world and contribute to the common good. Why not hold yourself up and celebrate yourself for all that you bring to this world? By listing out and documenting all the skills, talents, knowledge and wealth of experiences you have, at this time in your life, you are honoring yourself and building your sense of empowerment. That sense of empowerment is important for the next step in the Pause and Rediscover Process. Rediscovering your mission and purpose in this life and writing a vision statement for your next chapter.

## Exercise 4: Identify Your Mission and Purpose

Your mission is the reason you are here. Your purpose in this life. Your personal reason for being. It is what you are called to do from the heart, from deep inside of you. For example, my mission/purpose has been to be a family physician and be of service to others, as well as to have a family and raise my children to be successful, caring and compassionate human beings. Your purpose could be to be of service to your community or to be a leader in your profession. It may be to effect positive change in the world, to teach others life skills, design new structures that are green, or protect people in the event of a natural disaster or to raise a family.

There is no right or wrong purpose, simply a calling or feeling of what you are here to do or be in this lifetime. This part of the process can take a little time for you to be able to vocalize and embrace your mission/purpose, so give yourself some space and time to reflect and hone in on your reason for being. The reason I call this rediscovery is because we often voiced our purpose, or at least felt it when we were in our teens or as a young adult. It was part of our dreams for our future. The secret things we would share with only a few close friends or family or write down in a journal or diary. Over time you may have strayed from your mission or purpose. There are many factors that can contribute to that happening. For example, financial needs, family obligations, a medical illness for yourself or a family or loved one, or a natural disaster. Life can be complex at times, and you may change your path based on a whole variety of reasons. By pressing pause for just a bit you can rediscover your purpose and mission in life, and if you have drifted, find a way to get back to what is essential for you. Take a few minutes to write down all the things you feel you were called to do in this life. What do you sense is the reason you are here? Can you take those thoughts and narrow them down to a short 3–5-word sentence? Try to find the simplest way to describe your purpose at its essence. For example, "making a positive impact," "being of service to others," "creating connections across the community," creating beauty as an artist." This work may take you a while to process through and you may need some time to get to your core purpose or mission. It may help to step away and go for a walk, debrief with someone you trust, and then come back to complete the exercise and define your purpose.

## Exercise 5: Create Your Vision Statement

Once your purpose or mission is identified it is time for you to write a vision statement. This statement does not have to be lengthy or include everything thing you hope to do in your life. It should be one to two sentences long and be action oriented. It should be bold and big. When we complete this exercise in the business world, we look out over the next 3-5 years into the future and declare what the organization will be and do. Don't play small here, the sky is the limit, and this is your opportunity to look at all that you have described for yourself and feel empowered to create an audacious and courageous vision for your life.

This past year, my vision was to open my own growth and wellness company and publish a book. That is correct, I decided to do this at sixty years of age, with no background in book publishing, blogging, or setting up a website. I had never been self-employed or started a company. I still created that statement for myself and went bolder than I have in the past. And yes, I am working towards those goals and making progress in achieving that vision for myself. I never thought I would be an author ten years ago. Who was I to think that I could be an author? Well, why not me? Why not you, if that is your vision for yourself? I made a conscious decision to adopt a mindset of abundance and go for it! I had not understood that I had been stuck in a mindset of scarcity until I had the time to step back and reflect on my life and my choices. As you move through the following chapters in this book, I will share more on how to let go of old ways of seeing yourself and the world. To embrace your infinite possibilities and let go of scarcity thinking. I must admit that my journey has not been an easy one, and there has been so much for me to learn. And a hell of a lot of personal growth. There has also been more joy and a sense of empowerment than I have felt in many years.

What is your vision for yourself for the next 3-5 years? Where do you want to go and what do you want to achieve? Be big, be bold, be brave. If it feels too overwhelming to write down just yet, envision how it will feel when you achieve what is in your mind and heart. Where do you feel or sense it in your body? How do you want to feel? Start there and then as you feel able, go back to writing down the key components of your vision. It doesn't have to be in sentence format at first. You can jot down key bullet points for yourself on what it feels like, what it includes for you, and when you are ready, you can come back to that list and create your 2-3 sentence vision statement. It generally takes a few attempts to describe it in 2-3 sentences, so be gentle with yourself. Take the time you need to listen to your inner voice and look at the work you completed above to help craft your statement.

Congratulations! In this chapter you pressed pause from your busy life and took the time to reflect and rediscover the most important aspects of who you are. You identified your core values, the standards and principles by which you choose to act and behave in your life. You defined what you are passionate about and documented your unique set of skills, talents, knowledge and experiences. You clarified your purpose, your reason for being or mission, and created a vision statement for the future you. Great job!! This work is crucial in setting the foundation for the next step in the POWER UP transformation model.

# Chapter 1
# POWER POINTS

- Core values are the standards or principles by which we act or behave. Understanding your core values is a key component of personal and professional development. They act as a compass for your life.
- Your passions fuel your sense of fulfillment and joy. Make sure they are aligned with your work and personal life.
- You are the only you on this planet and have unique skills and talents to share with the world. These are your unique superpowers. Give yourself credit for all that you are and can do.
- Your purpose or mission is your reason for being. It is as unique as you are. Celebrate and embrace it!
- Creating a vision statement for your life can help empower you and provide a tangible resource for you to use in decision making, both in your personal and in your professional life.

# CHAPTER 2

## OBSERVE

### Be aware of your choices and current reality

*"Awareness is all about restoring your freedom to choose what you want instead of what your past imposes on you."*
Deepak Chopra

WHAT IF YOU OBSERVED YOUR CURRENT LIFE AND REALITY AS A scientist might and studied all the facts about your present situation in a very objective way. Would you find a difference between what you rediscovered about yourself in chapter one; your core values, passions, purpose, and vision for yourself, with where you are at the current time? What would your observations teach you about yourself? What questions would that raise for you?

To observe is "to come to realize or know especially through consideration of noted facts," or "to make a scientific observation," according to the Merriam Webster Dictionary. The definition also defines "observe" as another verb, to "watch carefully especially with attention to details or behavior for the purpose of arriving at a judgment." If you were a scientist, what would you find if you truthfully and very objectively observed your life's choices, your current state and present reality? Would it align well with what you described for yourself in chapter one?

Life tends to be unpredictable. We make plans for ourselves, dream of where we want to be and what we want for our lives. And then life unexpectedly steps in and hands us a challenge or unanticipated turn of events we never saw coming. For example, I had a patient who had dreamed of helping others and raising a family. She worked in a call center that supported emergency medical services and physicians after hours and loved her job. She became pregnant with her first child and was thrilled to give birth to a daughter. Then the unthinkable happened. She was diagnosed with pancreatic cancer and had only months to live. She never gave up on her vision for herself. She continued to live with purpose, despite being hospitalized until her death. She created multiple videos to share with her daughter as she grew older and passed milestones such as the first day of school, graduating high school, and her wedding day. Her life ended way too early, yet she remained happy and focused on her healing and purpose until the end. She was an inspiration to many of us who cared for her. She never strayed from her purpose and vision.

In my example, I had my entire life planned out for myself by the age of fifteen. I was going to attend Union College near my hometown, then go on to Albany Medical School, complete a Family Residency program at Albany Medical Center, get married and have three children. I had planned that by the time I was thirty I would be a successful physician. I would be married and raising a family, and I would be serene, balancing my life and work with ease. Sounds perfect, right?

Now for the facts. I was accepted to Union College and chose not to attend as I could not afford housing and would have had to live at home. Not an option for me, as my mother had mental illness and a substance abuse disorder, and home was anything but calm. It was very chaotic and dysfunctional, not an acceptable or satisfactory setting for me to study and achieve my goals. Instead, I went to a small college four hours from home where I was granted a scholarship. I then changed to the local state university the following year as the tuition was significantly less, and I was paying my own way. Medical school? I was introduced to Osteopathic Medicine while at the state university, and once I discovered it and its holistic focus, I decided I could only be an osteopathic family physician. The osteopathic philosophy of the body's ability to heal itself, and the connectedness of the mind, body and spirit resonated with me. I ended up in an osteopathic medical school in Maine, where I met my husband on day number three of school. We married two years later. I ended up in southern New Jersy for my residency program, to be close to my husband while he trained in Philadelphia. I never expected to live in southern New Jersey, but that was where I "matched" for my family medicine residency. When I turned thirty, I was back in Maine as a new faculty member and family physician at the medical school I had attended. I was also pregnant with our first child and trying to balance a busy work schedule with my husband's.

Oh, and we were also caring for his mother who was ill with a rare form of Parkinson's Disease. She needed full-time companion care, and she and the caretakers lived with us full-time. My life was anything but serene or what I had imagined it to be at the age of fifteen. Life provided challenges, including finances and family members with health issues. It also offered opportunities such as meeting my husband at a medical school I had never heard of until I was a senior in college. I made choices based on those challenges and opportunities, as well as the needs of my partner and family, and ended up in a different place than I had imagined for myself. If I observed the facts of my life objectively and bounced them off what I had envisioned for myself - my purpose, passion, values and talents, I was close. I was a family physician (purpose) married, had started a family, was caring for a loved one, and taught medical students and taking on additional responsibilities as the university clinic's medical director (skills and talents). I was able to be a healer, teacher, and leader as I had envisioned for myself. I was in a strong relationship with my life partner and supporting his family in a meaningful way as we built our careers and our family.

Fast forward a few decades. I am a senior leader in a health

JACKIE CAWLEY, DO, MBA

system and aspire to become its next chief medical officer. I am asked by my CEO to take on more responsibility in a different part of the organization for about a year. The term lasts seven years and I have a new boss who is very different from the one I have had for the previous five years. She does a reorganization that marginalizes me and several of my peers. She is not always honest. I am asked to stay and help in the department and given a new role, even though it means passing up the opportunity to be the health system's next chief medical officer. I work long hours and have limited time for self-care and exercise. I juggle family life with work, and not consistently very well. I find it hard to juggle my roles as a physician executive, mother, wife, daughter, friend and sister. I step back and objectively look at my current state and compare it to my core values, passions, purpose, skills and talents. The findings are not very pretty.

The new boss does not have the same values as I do. I am less passionate about the work I am doing as it becomes more restricted and routine. It is not the transformational work I have been leading for the health system for the past several years. My new role does not take advantage of my skills and talents. I am often exhausted by the long and less satisfying work hours, and have less time to spend with my young adult children and husband. I have minimal time for myself to rest and recharge. This is not what I had envisioned for myself.

There was a big disconnect between what I most cared about, who I was as a person and my life situation. I made the choice to make a change. I began a master's program in Business Administration and looked for another job in a different organization. One with values that were more aligned with mine and a role that would take full advantage of all that I had to offer. I found a fantastic position in a larger organization whose values resonated with my own, and a mission I was passionate about. To celebrate our family took a vacation to reconnect. We all decided it was our best family vacation ever.

The change allowed me to get back on track with my purpose, passions, and vision for my life as a physician executive. It required me to objectively observe where I was and what I wanted in my life. Without that intentional decision to observe my life like the medical scientist I was trained to be, I would not have been clear on how much I had drifted from my intentions for my life. How far I was from where I really wanted to be at this point in my life and my career.

What would you find if you looked objectively at your life right now, and compared it to what you described for yourself in chapter one? Would you be doing what you were passionate about? Would you be sharing your unique skills and talents with the world? Would you be in a place that aligned with your most essential core values as a human being?

Objectivity is important here. This exercise is not about judging your choices. It is about being truthful about what you desire most for yourself and your life and understanding where you currently are. In the business world we call this doing a Gap Analysis. It is part of the strategic planning process where we define our mission; or our reason for being. We then develop a vision for what we want to achieve as an organization and what we want to be known for. This is followed by an analysis of the current state and a comparison to our desired state in the future. This produces what we call our Gap Analysis. The Gap Analysis shows us what we have to change, add, or let go of to move to that new, future state.

You can do the same thing by comparing your current reality to what your desire most for yourself, based on the work you did in the first chapter. If you look objectively at your life, what do you find? How close or disparate is what you envisioned for yourself and where you are right now? Remember, you need to act like a scientist and just record the facts.

The whole purpose of this observation process is to become more aware of where you are, and how aligned it is with what you most want for yourself in this life. This awareness allows you to be more conscious of your reality and how it measures up to what you had dreamt of and hoped for yourself. The more well-defined your Gap Analysis, the easier it is to then move to the next step in the POWER UP transformation process, asking a very simple question, "Why." Why did you stray from your plans and dreams? What were the reasons you made certain decisions? Awareness of the gaps can be uncomfortable, but that is okay. This self-discovery and development work will be messy at times. It also will be empowering and transformative for you.

Use the prompts below to help you describe the facts about your current reality:

- *What is your current job or role?*
- *Where are you living and in what kind of environment?*
- *Do you feel your values align with those of your boss or company? With your partner? With your friend group?*
- *Do you spend time doing the things you are passionate about?*
- *How do you spend your time?*
- *Have you decided to compromise in some aspect of your life? What was that choice and the outcomes for you?*

Now let's go back and read what you created in Chapter One. Compare and contrast the work you completed in the first chapter with what you answered to the questions above. Act as a scientist would and record all the facts that you can observe. Do not judge what you observe. Just record it as objectively as you can. If you look impartially at what you wrote and listed as facts, what do you find? Is there any disconnect for you? Have you identified anything that surprises you? How close or far from your purpose or vision for yourself is your current reality?

Use this process to critically study your current reality and assess it against what you developed and described for yourself in Chapter One. In addition, study how you feel as you move through this exercise. What emotions does it bring forward for you? Where in your body do you feel these emotions? It is very important to record all that you observe as well as what you feel as you do this work. This will help you with the next step in the transformation framework, discovering your "why."

# Chapter 2
# Power Points

- Observation allows you to look at the facts of your life like a scientist.
- The facts you discover provide you with objective information and bring awareness to your current reality.
- A Gap Analysis of where you are vs. what you had described for yourself in Chapter One can be completed by comparing your present state with your desired life.
- To observe does not mean to judge, only to look at the facts and record them.
- This level of awareness can be uncomfortable and that is okay. The discomfort allows you to uncover the "why" of your choices in life.

# CHAPTER 3

# WONDER

## Discover how you got here

*"Owning our story and loving ourselves is
the bravest thing we will ever do."*
*Brene Brown*

IN THE LAST CHAPTER YOU WENT THROUGH AN EXERCISE TO objectively look at your life and compare it to the vision statement you created for yourself in Chapter One. Now, it is time to dig deep and identify what prompted you to make decisions along the way. It is time for you to wonder, to be curious, and discover how you got to this present place. To wonder is to be open to possibilities, to desire to know more and to be open to surprise.

When you study your life and the reasons for your decisions, it can be very enlightening. It brings to your conscious mind the logic or justification for making those decisions. What you find may surprise you. There are often outdated beliefs that we carry with us from childhood into adulthood. Our beliefs impact our actions and behaviors, so you need to be aware of the stories you carry with you. These can impact our decision making as adults and lead us astray from what we really want for ourselves. It is not always easy to find the root cause of our behaviors or decisions without taking the time to reflect and question "why."

In health care decisions are made daily that can impact a patient's life and wellbeing. The results of those actions or decisions can be disastrous and end up as an adverse event, negatively impacting a patient's care or their safety. That is one of the reasons we focus so much on improving quality and patient safety. To improve the quality and safety of patient care we often use a process called the **5 *Whys*** to determine the root cause of a problem or an adverse event. The **5 Whys** is a process improvement method to get to the root cause of an issue or problem. It is used in many industries and was made popular by Toyota in the 1970s. It is a simple technique to use and can help identify possibilities to consider rather than provide a solution. It has been invaluable to us in health care to improve patient safety and reduce adverse events.

An adverse event is when something does not go as planned and resulted in some type of injury to the patient. By asking the question "Why?" repeatedly for several rounds, the source of the problem or issue can be identified. Once identified, that root cause or source of the problem can be better understood. Once better understood, a change in the process of care or in the workflow can be made to improve the clinical care process. This should result in a better patient outcome. The goal is to improve the process so that the adverse event does not occur again.

The same approach can be used by an individual to uncover the basis or root cause of a problem or issue in their life. You can apply a similar method to your own life in order to understand how your present situation is different from the one you had imagined for yourself in Chapter One. It can help you identify where and when you made decisions that pushed you towards a different path than you may have planned for, and more importantly why you made the choices you did. By asking "Why?" you can discover the limiting beliefs you may have about yourself. It may uncover your fears, and any restrictions or constrictive expectations that you or your family and friends have developed for you. It will help you uncover the learned behaviors that you adopted to be accepted by others. Your actions that would be rewarded or to help you "fit in." It will bring forward to your consciousness the "Why" you act as you do in certain situations and the "Why" of how you have made decisions in your life.

The process is a simple one. It can also be uncomfortable as well as empowering for you, as you learn more about yourself and why you have made certain critical life decisions. That is part of the process. It is very hard for us in health care to witness adverse events, and our role in their cause. By using this process to get to the root cause changes can be implemented to decrease the chances of that mistake happening to another patient. The pain of acknowledging what went wrong can be tempered by the knowledge a change was made to improve care. Likewise, uncovering your "whys" may bring up strong emotions for you. This is okay and part of the work. Once those root causes and reasons are brought to your consciousness, you can actively make changes in how you view yourself and your life. You can be empowered to change your negative self-talk to positive self-talk. You can modify your behavior and your actions. You can reset your expectations for yourself and let go of the ones that have been limiting you from reaching your goals and being your best authentic self. How cool is that!

To begin this exercise, look back at the objective observations you discovered in the last chapter and the gaps between your present situation and what you had envisioned for yourself in Chapter One. What problems or issues have you identified for yourself? Be clear on what problem or issue you would like to solve and write it down at the top of a page of paper or on your favorite device. You may have seven things identified, and that is ok too. Start with one and then you can repeat this exercise for each problem or issue you have identified. Once you have a problem statement clearly defined it is time to begin the **5 Whys** process.

# 5 Why Exercise:

Write your problem statement or issue at the top of the page

## Ask yourself the first "Why?"

*Why is what you have identified above a problem or issue for you?*

Be as detailed and as truthful as possible. Being honest and owning your story is a critical to learning how to love and accept yourself completely. It allows you to understand all of who you are, including your shadow side. The answer you write down is not right or wrong; it just is a fact based on your decisions made with the best information you had at the time. And based on the best outcome you felt you would have by making that decision. There was never malintent on your part. Life happens and presents us all with challenges and decisions to be made as we navigate adulthood. We do the best we can at the time we make those decisions. Choices based on the information we have at our disposal, and what we feel is in the best interest of ourselves and others. Do not judge what you feel or what you discover. Just write it down.

Being honest with yourself allows you to make changes in the future and brings to light your shadow side. Your shadow side is the part of you that you try to hide from the world. We all have a shadow side, and we tend to want to hide that side from others and ourselves. The part of us that we are afraid to share with others because we might not be accepted or loved, or because we feel shame, guilt, and a sense of feeling "less than." Trying to keep that shadow side in the dark inhibits you from dealing with those negative feelings. It keeps you from replacing stale and limiting societal beliefs and negative self-talk with more healthy and positive ones. Bringing that side of you to light allows you to have a better sense of what makes you human. It helps you see why you have made some of the choices that you have in the past. It can be very enlightening and educational. You can use those lessons to learn from as you move into the future. Your shadow side is a wonderful teacher and guide, so do not shy away from your shadow side as you delve into the **5 Whys**. Embrace all of who you are and what makes you human and uniquely you.

Once you uncover the first reason "Why?", ask the question again.

## Ask "Why?" a Second Time.

Whatever you wrote down in answer to Why number one, ask yourself why you wrote that down. It may feel a bit foolish at first, but it helps to peel back the layers of your life decisions and get to the root causes. There is a reason for the answer you described with the first "Why?" Take your time to really dig deep and be honest with what comes to mind as you uncover the origins of your issue or situation.

Now go deeper and ask "Why?" a third time. "Why?" number three applies to your answer to the second one. Repeat this line of questioning "why" for your answers a fourth time, and finally a fifth time. What have you uncovered about yourself and how you have made your life decisions? The answers may surprise you. They will certainly help you better understand your decision-making process and any impacts created by your shadow side. It will help to bring this to your consciousness. Once you are conscious of the information you can adjust or change your actions, behaviors, and self-talk.

Here is a simple example of how this technique works. Let's say the problem is arriving at work several minutes late most of the time. Ask the first why. From this, you determine it is because you took longer to get ready than you had planned for yourself. Now ask why a second time: why did it take longer to get ready than anticipated? The answer is that you tried on three different outfits before picking one you wanted to wear. Ask Why a third time: why did you have so many outfits to try on? You decide it is due to not planning. Time for the forth why: why had you not planned? You were busy watching Netflix and scrolling on your phone the night before. Now ask the fifth and final why: why not plan rather than spend time on the phone and watching television? You deduce it is because you did not want to think about work in the evening. Terrific.

You have identified that you do not plan ahead, which tends to make you late to work. You do not want to spend your free time planning for the next workday. What are your options? Option 1: Set the alarm for ten minutes earlier in the morning, to give yourself more time to try on outfits. Option 2: Take ten minutes before bed to lay out a few wardrobe options for ease of trying on in the morning. Option 3: Spend Sunday afternoon picking out five work outfits and place them in a handy spot in your closet to grab one in the morning. You decide to go with Option 3.

Below is an example of how I have applied the **"5 Whys"** process to my life, which may help you better understand how to complete this exercise for yourself.

## My 5 Whys Process

Problem Statement:

I made the decision to stay in a role I was unhappy with, and with a boss who had very different values from my own.

**"Why?" Number One:**

I agreed to take the initial leadership role when my CEO asked me to help the health system with a major project because I wanted to make him happy and demonstrate that I was loyal to him and the organization. When he asked me to stay there, I did so because I wanted him to be pleased with me. It showed me that he felt I was doing a good job, even though I did not feel it was the best working situation for me. I liked the external recognition and being considered a "good" leader.

**"Why?" Number Two:**

I wanted my CEO to be happy because I tend to be a people-pleaser and overachiever. I felt the need for external recognition in order to feel valued.

Okay. This made sense to me. I was the oldest child in a very dysfunctional family and took the role of being responsible for my younger siblings. I tried to be "good" to make things less chaotic at home. I tried to please my parents to help reduce the stress and tension in the household. I tried to be good as a child at home and school to feel better about myself and get approval. It made me feel more in control of my life and recognized. It also resulted in my being an overachiever. I can see this as being a factor in my decision making in my adult life.

**"Why?" Number Three:**

Why did I feel the need to make my CEO happy? Why did I need external gratification? Ouch! Here it gets a bit uncomfortable. It was all about wanting acceptance. I wanted to make him happy so that he would accept and value me. I needed external validation rather than trusting my own internal approval.

**"Why?" Number Four:**

I needed external approval and validation because I was afraid. I feared my CEO and others seeing the "real me." I worked hard to meet other people's desires and needs and often sacrificed my own to be accepted. I was afraid if they saw the "real me" I would not be accepted into the "club." That is what we (my fellow women peers and I) called the C-suite of predominately white men in the organization. They were the powerful ones in the organization and made all the critical decisions.

**"Why?" Number Five:**

Why was I afraid? I felt that I was an imposter and not good enough for the roles that I had been given. I did not feel I was enough, and I felt shame. I was afraid to say the wrong thing, be humiliated, or not be accepted.

Ugh. This was getting messy. This was getting real. I was starting to feel a yucky sensation in my stomach. Why had I handed my power to others and where did this fear of not being enough come from? Had I all along been making choices in my personal and professional life based on this underlying root cause? Unfortunately, yes I had, and I had not been conscious of that fact.

The process of the **5 Whys** made me uncomfortable. It also brought to light my shadow tendency of looking for external validation. The tendency to be focused on pleasing others rather than myself, and a sense of feeling "not good enough." This was despite being a successful physician executive and being seen by others as a strong and competent leader. Inside, I felt "not good enough." By uncovering the basis of my decision making I was able to bring to light, and to my consciousness, my shadow tendencies. My shadow tendency is to look to others for approval rather than trusting myself and giving myself my own internal approval. Another is being afraid of not being accepted, not being loved, not being enough. Those feelings had real foundations from my childhood. And let's face it, the need to have a sense of belonging is one of Maslow's basic elements in his *Hierarchy of Needs*. It is right there after food, water, shelter, and safety. You cannot move up the hierarchy until the first levels have been fulfilled. Until I was sure I belonged and was accepted by the executive leadership at work, I could not move to a feeling of self-confidence and self-esteem.

## Figure 3: Maslow's Hierarchy of Needs

SELF-
ACTUALIZATION
morality, acceptance,
existence, purpose, meaning,
creativity, inner potential

SELF-ESTEEM
confidence, achievement, respect of
others, need to be unique individual

LOVE AND BELONGING
friendship, family, intimacy, sense of connection

SAFETY AND SECURITY
health, employment, property, family and social ability

PHYSIOLOGICAL NEEDS
breathing, food, water, shelter, clothing, sleep

My desire to belong and be accepted is not unique. The desire to belong and to connect with others is a universal human need. We are social beings. Social interaction is fundamental to our health and wellbeing, and we are basically biologically hard-wired for connection and relationships with others. This need for acceptance and belonging is something we become conscious of around the age of four or five. At that age we notice if others are unhappy with us, or with something that we did. We become aware that the adults we love, and trust do not always approve of all our actions. They tell us to quiet down. To stay still. To hurry up. To get dressed, but "wait, not that outfit!"

It is not always verbal. It may be a frown, a lifted eyebrow, or a shake of the head. It could be a sigh when we make a mistake, do not meet expectations, or or cannot easily achieve what another child can easily do. We experience our peers not picking us for kickball teams or letting us sit at their table at lunchtime. Yes, this happened to me.

Our basic human desire to belong is so strong that we begin to blame ourselves when others do not accept us or are unhappy with us. That is when we learn to feel less than, not "good enough," and even shame. As a result, we adapt to make sure we are accepted. We change how we act, what we say and what we do to fit in. We create stories about ourselves that become our beliefs. Over time we internalize these stories and beliefs and begin to doubt ourselves. We do what we feel is necessary to be accepted, belong and be loved.

Without a sense of belonging and feeling love and acceptance, one cannot move to self-esteem. Self-esteem is when you have self-confidence. Confidence in your own self-worth and you respect yourself. When I look back at that time in my life when I was doing the right thing" for my CEO, and staying in a role I was unhappy in, I can clearly see that I was still suffering from imposter syndrome and still did not feel completely confident in my skills. I did not feel accepted for my authentic self and what I brought to the organization. I suffered from a sense of low self-esteem.

That shadow side can be a wonderful teacher. The lesson for me was to figure out why I behaved and felt that way. What limiting expectations of others or limiting beliefs did I have that resulted in my life decisions? In my feeling "not enough" or being an imposter in my executive role? In needing external validation rather than being okay with and trusting my own internal recognition? It was based on my narrative, my personal story that I had created for myself as a younger person. The one that I had adopted in my subconscious, stored in my memory banks, and which influenced my actions and decisions, even as a mature and successful adult. The good thing is that once the shadow side is brought to light, you can address it and make changes. What is learned can be unlearned. What I adopted as my story and set of limiting beliefs as a young child and adolescent could be replaced with a new set of healthier, more positive and empowering ones.

Try the **5 Whys** process for yourself. Be as honest as you can be as you delve deep into your reasons for behaving and making the decisions you have made. Your shadow tendencies can be very enlightening and help you identify why you have strayed from your life purpose, north star, and vision for yourself. You may get to the root cause by round four of the process, or it may take a few extra rounds to get to the source of your decisions and behaviors. Keep asking to get to the actual root cause.

The important thing is to draw forth the underlying reasons of why you do what you do. The basis for your actions. The reasons you are where you are, and why you have made the decisions in your life that you have. The ones that have resulted in your present set of circumstances. Once those are uncovered, you must own them. You must take complete responsibility and accountability for your choices and actions and embrace all that you have uncovered. Then you can move to the next step in the POWER UP transformation model. To expose and express the limiting beliefs and societal expectations you have adopted for yourself. To clearly reveal the narrative or story you have told yourself. Until that narrative is exposed and expressed you cannot bring it to your conscious awareness and make a change. Once you are aware of the story you have been telling yourself and how it does not make sense for the person you are right now, you can let it go. You can replace it with a more positive, aligned and empowered set of beliefs.

# Chapter 3
# POWER POINTS

- The **5 WHYs** method can help get to the root cause of a problem or situation.

- Getting to the root cause of why you make decisions in your life can be messy and sometime uncomfortable, However, that is part of the process of learning and owning your decisions and present life situation.

- Your shadow side can be an excellent teacher. Bring your shadow side to light so that you can learn from your past choices and shadow tendencies.

- Once you uncover the root cause or basis for your decisions in life, it is important to own them fully. You made decisions and are living with the consequences of those decisions.

- Your decisions have not been right or wrong, they were simply the result of your making the best decision based on the information you had at the time. That includes your adopted narrative, and what you felt was in the best interest of all involved.

# SECTION TWO
# POWER PLAY

*"The real difficulty is to overcome how you think about yourself"*
*Maya Angelou*

# CHAPTER 4

# EXPOSE

## Become conscious of your limiting beliefs

*"Most people are living an illusion based on someone else's beliefs."*
Jen Sincere
*You are a Badass*

OUR BRAIN AND OUR NERVOUS SYSTEM ARE REMARKABLE AND VERY complex. We take in a tremendous amount of information as we experience the world around us, acquiring data through our five senses. We do this twenty-four hours a day, every day, for our entire life. Information or data that then needs to be processed and made sense of each second of the day. Our brain functions to keep us safe and alive and tries to make sense of the world as we take in the immense amount of information our body senses. To transmit all of that data from our sensory organs, such as our eyes, mouth and nose, and skin, we have specialized nerve cells. These nerve cells are called neurons which turn what we feel, smell or taste into small chemicals called neurotransmitters, and into electrical connections. These neurochemicals and the electrical connections and interactions allow the brain to receive that sensory information and then make sense of it for us.

Ten percent of our brain is made up of these neurons, and there are approximately 86 billion of them in our brain and nervous system. In addition, each neuron communicates with around 1,000 other neurons. Think about how many overall connections there are. It is mind boggling. This system of neurons turns our sensations into chemical and electrical signals that pass from cell to cell. This communication system allows our brain to take what we sense and think and turns that data into something we can process and respond to. It is like a giant complex set of highways that help us experience the world, process and then deliver that data to our subconscious and conscious mind. Some of those neural highways or pathways get a lot of traffic, while others get less traffic. The more a pathway is used, the easier it is for the mind to use that same pathway in the future. It is like creating a new trail in a meadow. The more it is traveled, the deeper the trail becomes. The better the path, the easier it is for someone to use it. The pathways in our brain and nervous system work in a similar manner. That will be an important point to remember as you move forward in this journey.

Our brain houses our conscious mind, which we use for making decisions, solving problems, and making logical sense of our reality. It may surprise you to know that it is related to only about 3% of our brain activity, which means the conscious mind is only the tip of the iceberg when we think about our overall consciousness. Which does not seem to make sense when we live in our conscious state all day long. However, it is true, only 3% of our brain's activity is related to what we think about and consciously do all day long.

We also have a subconscious brain that works in the background to take in all the data we sense, feel or think, and stores it in our memory. It is a giant storage bank of data that is related to about 95% of the activity in our brain. Its job is to help protect us from all kinds of danger, physical as well as emotional danger. For the subconscious mind, it cannot tell an emotional danger apart from a real physical one. It simply tries to keep us alive and safe. It is also responsible for all the automatic functions happening in our body. It keeps our heart beating, our digestive tract working and our breathing continues, in an unconscious way.

Remember all the trillions of data points coming into and being processed by your brain and nervous system? That complex set of electrical and chemical highways and pathways? That data is being processed and categorized continually by our subconscious mind. That is why 95% of our brain activity is used by the subconscious mind. It works in the background and uses symbols, emotions, and other stored memory to help it let go of data we do not need and to actively respond and dish up information to our conscious mind when there is a perceived danger or something we need to actively address. It may be a real danger, or it can also be somewhat distorted based on how we have stored memory in the past. For example, say you step into the path of a moving vehicle. You did not the car see as you began to cross the street. Your subconscious mind notes the vehicle and sends that information to your consciousness. Now you can make the decision to jump out of the car's way in just a fraction of a second. Or perhaps you may notice a slender, dark object in your peripheral vision. Your subconscious mind may distort it so that your brain interprets that it may be a snake instead of a stick. Your conscious mind then helps you to decide what to do. You look more closely and realize you are safe. It is simply a stick on the sidewalk. Your entire history of previous experiences and emotions all play into that split second decision.

The brain and nervous system are busy 24/7/365 ensuring we are safe. Taking data from our five senses, our emotions, and thoughts, and figuring out a way to process, assess and categorize that data. Then, it can be interpreted and stored or acted upon. The way in which we do this is unique for each person. Everyone has a different way of experiencing the world and categorizing that data in their brain. As we experience the world, we learn. We continually take in information and store it in our memory banks for future use, when and if we need it.

For example, when we are toddlers and we reach for the stove, and are told it is "hot" and to "move away." If we do not follow the direction to move away, we experience pain. We learn to associate a stove with "hot" and the sensation of pain, and act differently after that. We avoid touching a hot stove to avoid pain. In much the same way, we learn about our whole world. That complex system of neurons takes all our data and over time, through our experiences and the unique way we each store and categorize information, we create our story. Our personal narrative of how we see and experience the world and how we perceive ourselves. This narrative or story influences how we think and how we act.

Why is this important? In the last chapter you took the time to ask why you have made certain choices in your life. Why you acted or reacted in certain ways to better understand how you have arrived at a place in your life that may be incompatible with your values, passions and purpose. Generally, it is because of how your narrative has influenced your decision making. As you learn and grow as a child and adolescent, you make judgments and have experiences that affect your decision making and actions in the future. For example, perhaps you are afraid of public speaking. Each time you are asked to speak in public, you get a sick feeling of fear in your stomach and try to find a way out of doing so. Why? Your brain, at some point in the past, stored a set of data that equated public speaking as dangerous. If you go back in time to when you first felt that way, you may uncover it was related to the time you stumbled going to the front of the room to present your book report in the fourth grade, and the other children laughed at you. If that experience made you feel embarrassed and ashamed, then the next time a similar situation is identified by your subconscious mind, it responds by sending a "hey, this is a danger" message to your body and conscious mind, and you may respond by saying no or making an excuse to get out of that scenario. You don't consciously recall the initial event from fourth grade; your emotions simply kick into gear based on the stored memory and your subconscious mind sends an alert message to your conscious mind that it could be a hazardous situation for you and should be avoided.

What is amazing is that if we can identify what the limiting belief or story we create for ourselves we can use those same neural pathways to create a new story or narrative. One that is more aligned with our current reality as adults. For example, the fear of public speaking described above. Once you can expose the initial event and express it to yourself, you can develop a new neural pathway and store it in your memory bank. You can use your conscious mind to tell yourself that you are a successful adult who enjoys speaking with people and is an expert in your field. By saying that aloud to yourself, writing it or thinking it repeatedly, you can create a new pathway in your subconscious mind that equates public speaking with the feeling of confidence in yourself as a subject matter expert who is happy to share your knowledge with others through public speaking.

When I went through the **5 Whys** in the last chapter, I identified that I felt like an imposter and was not confident in my abilities and skills. This was despite being a very successful physician leader. What was my set of limiting beliefs? My limiting narrative of myself? As a child living in a very chaotic home with a mom who had mental illness and substance abuse issues, I thought I could make things better and more stable at home if I was just "good enough." That might make sense if I am four or five years old and know that if I behave in a certain way that is seen as positive by people in authority or power, I am rewarded. If I sit quietly in church, I get a cookie afterwards. If I pick up my toys before bed, I get a positive response from my parents. If I scratch initials into the top of my parent's dresser, I get punished.

I began to apply that internal narrative for myself and kept trying to be good enough. I tried to be good enough all the time. At home, and at school. It was exhausting. It seemed logical at that age, so I processed and stored in my subconscious mind that I needed to be good so that home would be less crazy and chaotic. This narrative would then pop up for me when I faced similar situations as I grew older. Let's face it, life is full of surprises and new experiences. When I would experience something similar to what my five-year old brain interpreted as chaotic or stressful, my response was to be the "good girl." Get things taken care of, get good grades, say yes and take on the added responsibility. I just had to be "good" and all would be well. And that is what I did for most of my adult life. This resulted in having less than stellar boundaries and taking on more than I could handle well at work and at home. It also resulted in my feeling stretched too thin and stressed much of the time. Let's face it, it is not easy to be "good" all of the time.

I was unaware of how my past influenced my behavior and decision making. So, I stayed in a role with an awful boss to make my CEO happy. By uncovering the fact that I had been making decisions based on a limiting belief that had I stored in my brain as a five-year-old, I could see that this belief was not actually accurate. I could never be good enough to always make everyone else happy. It was not humanly possible. Once I was able to expose and express what was influencing my behaviors, actions, and decisions, I was able to see how I needed to change the way I behaved and how I made life choices going forward. The old narrative would not work for me or make sense for me as an adult. This then allowed me to reroute those neurochemical and electrical connections and lay down a new, more positive, and empowering narrative for myself.

I unlearned the old story and created a brand new one with data that made much more sense to my adult self. The new narrative was that I was enough. That I was a very successful and intelligent physician executive with skills and attributes to share with the world. My new narrative was one that allowed me to put healthy boundaries in place at work and at home. Rewiring those well-traveled neuronal highways and pathways took some time. I had to learn to be more aware of when the old story would pop into action and stop it consciously. To become more intentional about how I was making decisions and ensuring I enlisted my new way of experiencing the world, my new narrative, when faced with challenges and chaos.

I practiced meditation, yoga and saying positive affirmations daily to focus my conscious thoughts in a more positive way. When negative self-talk or a limiting belief popped into my head, I would consciously replace it with my new narrative. I would say positive statements aligned with my new storyline. Such as "I am enough," "I can totally do this," and" I am a strong and powerful person." One

40

of my favorites was, "I am grateful for the abundance and success that flows into my life with ease. A much better way to talk about myself. It took time and practice. Those new neural connections and interactions need to be traveled repeatedly to become the more automatic response when faced with a similar situation. Remember, the brain wants to conserve energy and take the easiest path possible to follow. All of this work is worth it. Not only does the new pathway result in a better outcome, it also results in better self-awareness, an important skill to build and strengthen as a leader and person. Being aware of how I was responding to the world, and what my limiting and outdated story was for myself allowed me to consciously unlearn that response and replace it with something that was a better fit for me in my current life.

You can do this as well. You can unlearn the parts of your story that no longer fit who you really are as an adult. You can reframe how your brain experiences the world, categorizes, and stores new information. In the last chapter you discovered your root cause or source for why your current reality does not align well with what you most want for yourself. What did you find as your underlying reason when you went through the **5 Whys** process? If you look at the source of your why, identified in the last chapter, what does this trigger for you?

- *What emotions does this bring up for you?*
- *What memories come forward to your consciousness?*
- *What sensations does this bring to you, and where do you feel them in your body?*
- *Can you expose your limiting beliefs or stories?*

When I exposed my source of why, it was uncomfortable for me. I felt shame of being found out as an imposter and fear of not being accepted. I felt a pit in my stomach. Looking back to my childhood, I felt that way at home when my mother was not well and acted oddly. I would feel the same way when my parents fought. If I look back far enough into the past I can see when, as a little girl, I decided I needed to be good so that all would be okay. And I would feel less sick to my stomach and less anxious.

If we look back to the example in the last chapter of being late to work, the root cause was due to a lack of planning. Perhaps planning ahead did not work out for you as a child or plans kept changing and you had to stay flexible. Or, perhaps you moved frequently as a child. Moving so often made it hard to make friends and establish roots. Maybe this made you feel anxious and uncomfortable, and you identified planning as something that is not helpful for you. As a result, you subconsciously decided not to plan where possible just to be safe. Now, you can see the old, outdated way of thinking about planning, and you can make a change in your behavior for the future.

Take a moment and go back to the exercise in the last chapter and look at to the fundamental reason for making certain critical decisions in your life. Can you go back to the very first time you felt the same or similar sensations and emotions you felt when thinking about your root cause?

- *What was happening then?*
- *What age were you?*
- *What was your environment like?*
- *What were the facts of the situation?*
- *Can you identify what triggered those sensations and feelings?*

Express as much as you can about how you feel, what you remember, and what was happening in your life at the time. This process can feel uncomfortable and that is expected. You are consciously returning to the essence and experience of that situation or time in your life when you laid down an event in your memory banks as a danger. When you created an emotional and physical response that was stored in your subconscious and pushed you out of your comfort zone. And it is the only way you can truly uncover the basis of your limiting or outdated belief, and way of experiencing the world and yourself. Take your time and be gentle with yourself. Give yourself some time to bring the subconscious part of you to light. The subconscious mind speaks to us in symbols, emotions, and through dreams and sensations. This occurs to bring what is deep in your memory banks to your awareness, your conscious mind. Mindfulness practices such as yoga, meditation and breathing exercises can prompt these old memories to arise unexpectedly. Don't judge yourself or how long it may take for you to complete this important step. Moving through this process will help you to feel more empowered. It will show you where you need to replace old ways of thinking with new, more powerful and positive ones. Once you expose and express these subconscious ways of thinking and reasoning, you can consciously step in and change for your current and future life.

# Chapter 4
## POWER POINTS

- We continuously take in data as we sense and experience the world, which is stored in our subconscious memory banks.
- Our brain and nervous system are made up of nerve cells that send chemical and electrical messages that create trillions of pathways and help our brain assess, categorize and store data.
- Our subconscious mind makes up 95% of our brain's activity and is there to keep us alive and out of danger.
- Our subconscious mind cannot tell the difference between physical and emotional danger. It uses emotions, symbols, and stored memory to make assessments and send messages to the conscious mind.
- Everyone is unique in how they sense, perceive and encounter the world, and how they categorize and store data.
- As we store data and experience the world, we create our unique story or narrative.
- That story or narrative is what influences our actions and decisions.
- The narrative begins to be laid down in early childhood and can consist of limiting beliefs that keep us from reaching our full potential.
- Once you know the belief or narrative that is limiting you, you can unlearn it and replace it with a new and more accurate one.

# CHAPTER 5

# REPLACE

## You have the power to rewrite your story

*"The secret to change is to focus all of your energy
not fighting the old, but on building the new"*
Socrates

YOU HAVE DONE AN AMAZING AMOUNT OF HARD WORK IN THE LAST few chapters. Awesome job! You have uncovered your purpose, values and what motivates and excites you. You have identified the root cause of how you got to where you currently are in your life, which may be different from what you had originally envisioned or planned for yourself. You have taken the time to expose and become consciously aware of your limiting beliefs and obsolete ways of perceiving yourself and experiencing the world. You have learned that the way you sense and encounter the world and yourself is based on the narrative or story that you developed internally over time. A narrative that began when you were a small child, and which was influenced by your family of origin, friends, loved ones, society, cultural and religious affiliations, teachers, coaches, etc. Your narrative is unique to you. And it was all learned. That means, it can be unlearned and replaced with a new, more modern, and updated version that better reflects who you are now as an adult.

As you become more aware of what has been limiting for you and keeping you from reaching your full potential and dreams, you become better able to label the feelings, emotions, thoughts, and outdated parts of your story. It is crucial to articulate and label these clearly, along with how and where in your body the emotions and beliefs are stored. That is your body's way of communicating with you when something is sensed by your subconscious as a possible danger. Remember, the subconscious is not able to tell if a danger is a physical one or emotional one, so it uses your body to signal and communicate to your conscious mind when it is alerted that something is possibly wrong or a threat to you. Your body responds the same way whether a danger is real or perceived. By understanding this concept and where and how your body reacts, you can use the body's communication signals to quickly be more conscious of your feelings and emotions. By being more aware of your emotions, feelings and reactions you can learn to easily identify, name and validate them.

Validating your emotions is essential. Your feelings and emotions are real, and it is okay to experience them and let them flow through you. Emotions and bodily sensations will not hurt you. It is just the way your brain interprets the data you take in, and helps you be more mindful of potential problems. Your brain trying to keep you safe and make sense of the world based on your unique narrative and set of past experiences. By being more conscious of your emotions and the "why" behind what you are feeling, you can thank your brain for trying to keep you safe. You can tell your brain and conscious mind know that the fear is not real. That you are safe. In fact, you can tell your brain that not only are you safe but that you got this!

For example, let's look at the fear of public speaking. When you start to feel that sinking pit in your stomach, or your throat closing off when asked to present to a group, you can politely and calmly thank your subconscious for trying to keep you safe from embarrassment. Like that time in the fourth grade when you tripped, and the class all laughed at you. Your conscious mind can tell your subconscious that you completely got this. You can inform your conscious mind that this is not the fourth grade anymore, and you are safe. In fact, you can tell your brain that you love to share your expertise with others. Even if it is not totally true yet. Your subconscious does not care. The conscious is the captain of your brain and whatever it tells your subconscious mind is taken as the truth. As you tell your brain this new fact, it creates new neuronal pathways of thinking and feeling in your brain. The more you use the new pathways, the more your brain will process that public speaking is not a scary, dangerous thing for you, but a positive experience.

That is how you begin to replace your old, and outdated ways of perceiving yourself and the world and let go of those limiting beliefs that have been holding you back from your most awesome and best self. You have the power to replace all that does not fit with where you are now in your life, and where you want to go in the future. The power is yours. You get to be the captain of your brain and tell it what you want it to do, feel and think. You can be the creator of those new neuronal cell communications and newly developed pathways in your brain. How cool is that! It does takes practice and being present. It does require you to be mindful and aware of your emotions, thoughts, and sensations. You must be willing to face those old fears and negative feelings or sensations and identify what caused them in the first place. Once they are exposed and expressed, you can swap them out with new, more positive, and empowering ones. Ones that are aligned with your values, passions, and purpose. It may take some time, and you can fake it until you make it stick! For example, you get a feeling of dread when you catch your reflection in a mirror, to yourself, "I look tired," "Too skinny," "Too heavy," "Silly in this outfit," or whatever negative sentence pops up all the time in your head. The dread you feel and its associated responses in your body are a signal to you to be more conscious of your thinking and emotions. How awesome is that! If you are more mindful of those thoughts and reactions you can stop yourself in mid-sentence and look yourself squarely in that mirror and replace the previous thought with a new, more encouraging, and affirmative one.

For example, here are some much more constructive and optimistic suggestions for you.

- *I am strong and confident.*
- *I am beautiful inside and out.*
- *I rock my new haircut.*
- *I look great in this outfit.*
- *I thank my body for all it does for me every day.*
- *I love my _____ (fill in whichever body part you feel best about here).*

Don't these statements feel much more empowering? Thinking and saying these phrases should result in a different set of responses in your body. You can make the impression on your mind even stronger by doing a fist pump in the air while you say the statement or by placing your hands on your hips, and leaning into your reflection in the mirror, and looking yourself in the eyes while you say the statement. Say it out loud. Sing it or add some dance moves. Whatever comes to mind. And yes, it may feel a bit awkward, uncomfortable, or silly at first. That is normal.

Remember, you have been saying negative things to yourself for a long time. Just keep at it. Those old pathways will be unlearned, and the new ones will become more natural and automatic over time. Our minds and bodies are connected, so gestures, movements, and even a simple smile can impact your brain perceives and processes. Try these few postures right now and see what happens in your emotions, thoughts, and body. Smile a big smile and look at yourself in a mirror. Now add a laugh or two. What do you feel? Where in your body do you feel it? Smiling sends signals to the brain and because a smile has been associated with feeling happy in the past, your brain equates the smile to your happiness. Right in the moment. Research has shown that smiling results in feeling happier and more positive. When you smile at someone else, they tend to smile as well. The mind and body are connected, so you can use your body to signal to the brain what you want to feel.

Let's try another posture. Stand up with your feet hip distance apart and place your hands on your hips. How does that feel? What emotions does this stance create for you? It makes me feel more powerful and strong. I can feel it in my solar plexus and my look becomes more determined if I look at myself in a mirror. What happened for you?

I have used this posture before a presentation or interview to help me feel more confident and powerful prior to walking into an interview room or Board room. Now raise a fist and shout out "Yes!" That gets me feeling pumped and excited every time. It is fun to do this with your team at a meeting, or when doing a presentation. Get people up and have them do a fist pump while saying a positive affirmation, and watch the change in the level of energy and number of smiles that result. The key is anchoring the new way of thinking by using your body in multiple ways. In the example above the use of gestures and postures along with your voice and seeing and hearing the others around you.

Yes. You need to repeat what you want to change to make it stick, and for the new pathways to be traveled more frequently in your brain. For example, negative self-talk when you walk by a mirror. You picked a new and more positive statement for yourself. Now be sure to say your new affirmations multiple times a day and add a physical gesture to help anchor it in your subconscious memory banks. Think or say it whenever you see your reflection. Do this several times a day for a few weeks. Over time and with practice, the negative feeling will go away and be replaced with a more constructive, encouraging, and more empowering sensation when you catch that glimpse of yourself in a mirror.

This deliberate and intentional replacement of the old negative self-talk with new more more inspiring one is entirely in your power. You have the power to unlearn the old narrative and replace it with a fresh one that you purposefully and consciously develop. All you must do is be willing to be open and listen to your body. To feel and name the emotions and sensations in your body and become more aware and conscious of what your subconscious mind is trying to alert you to. Use what you exposed in the last chapter to determine what is limiting and outdated, for you. Then, deliberately create a new narrative for yourself. A new, powerful and constructive statement for every negative or limiting thought and belief that has been keeping you from reaching your potential. You are the captain of your brain. Take control and have your conscious mind tell your subconscious what your new way of experiencing the world and yourself will be going forward.

You can start small with just one thing. One outdated and invalid thought or belief that you have and replace it with a powerful new way of feeling and thinking about yourself. Add a stance, facial expression or movement to anchor that revised belief or concept in your physical body. Practice this multiple times a day. Once that new mode of thinking has been anchored and more automatic for you, try the process again. You will build confidence in your ability to change the lens and reframe how you look at yourself. You will change how you think about yourself, and your self-talk. Your physical response when faced with the same or a similar challenge or situation in the future. Over time this new set of chemical and electrical connections and pathways in your brain will become more dominant. Your story will be rewritten and relearned. It will be replaced with your new, improved and more authentic narrative. You become what you think. You have the power to change your narrative.

You have power, and you have more power than you know. You just need to be open to it and own it. When you own your power, you act as your authentic self and speak your voice with grace and honesty. You recognize your strengths and unique gifts and have the confidence to achieve your personal and professional dreams and goals. You understand that we all have access to this wonderful sense of awareness of self and positive energy, and you lift others up to feel empowered as well. Yet, how many people genuinely feel empowered, or own their power and express it?

We often give our power away. We give our power to others who frighten, intimidate us or try to make us feel guilty. We give our power to those in authority. We give away our power to fit in or to avoid negative consequences from those who use their force to control others. Often times, we do not even recognize that we have ceded our power to another person. We are simply trying to keep the peace, keep others happy, and follow acceptable societal constructs and rules. We want to be accepted and part of the community. To be connected.

We question our right to step into our power. Unfortunately, we start with negative self-talk. Try this instead:

- *How can I own my power and shine my light?*
- *Who am I to shine my light?*
- *Who am I to speak with my authentic voice?*
- *What if they disagree with what I have to say?*
- *Isn't it safer to play small?*
- *Isn't it less risky to comply and not make waves?*

The result is our tendency to hide our true selves and give our power to those who are deemed more worthy, more experienced, intelligent, or in charge. I know I did. I gave my power to my bosses, my CEO, and my professors. I wanted to please others and be accepted. For example, I wanted to be seen as a high potential leader and have the opportunity to climb the leadership ladder. I wanted to be part of my organization's senior team. So, I went along with the decisions of my boss, and the directions from my CEO. I was helpful and supportive and receive an "exceeds expectations" at all my annual performance reviews. I would move from the boardroom conference table to make room for the "real" leaders and sit in the row of chairs along the windows. I thought that would give me points for being a team player. I was wrong. Others perceived my stepping back from the table to be a demonstration of my lack of self-confidence. That it showed I did not feel I was worthy of sitting at the table with the other executives. The result was a sense of being overworked, overburdened and frustrated. When I was passed by for a promotion, I took the opportunity to step back and reflect. To assess my actions, my behaviors, my accomplishments, my strengths and where I still had gaps. I realized I had spent much of my time making others, such as my boss, look good and be successful. I had made sure that I was seen as the go to "utility player" and loyal employee by leadership. Along the way, I forfeited my own ability to be promoted. I had given away my power and had not realized it. Well, at least not consciously.

I know that I had concerns that certain decisions did not align with my values. I knew I had innovative ideas that could help to transform our health system more quickly. I just could not get traction with them based on the overly conservative nature of some the senior team. I sensed that some of them felt I was too "soft" and too "caring" to make the "hard" decisions. One even made an offhand comment to that effect after a meeting we had both attended on a Friday afternoon. It was the meeting where the same individual commented about my outfit and my plans for the weekend. For them, what I wore and my role as a mother impacted my ability to be an effective leader. I had a gut feeling that my authentic leadership style was not aligned with those that I worked for. So, I chose to be more like the peers I worked with, who had embraced the predominant male model of power. The power construct adopted by our society for the past several millennia. I became very skilled at it, but it never felt quite right. I can even recall the exact day that the comment was made and my reactions and emotions when it happened.

It was a sunny summer day, and I was the medical staff president of a large medical center. I had worn a lovely, flowy, lavender dress that made me feel beautiful. When asked about weekend plans, I shared that I had a dance recital to attend, in which my daughter and I were dancing together. The individual laughed, and asked if I would give them a show. They went on and commented that my dress was not very business-oriented. I felt embarrassed by the statement. After that day I wore dark colored business suits, which I referred to as my "armor." Dressing every morning to feel more confident for whatever power struggle popped up and to be seen as a player, and more accepted by senior leadership.

What is really sad is that on that particular day, I stepped out of my car on my way to the meeting and felt a powerful surge of energy flow through me. It caught me off guard and surprised me. It also thrilled me and made me feel terrified at the same time. I embraced that sense of power as I walked into the meeting that afternoon and had a smile on my face. I felt optimistic and excited to chair the meeting. When that individual made the comment about my dress and dance plans, my sense of power drained away in a nanosecond. Along with it, my confidence. Suddenly, I felt like an imposter.

The meeting went well, and all the work was successfully accomplished. However, I felt deflated. Looking back on that day, I feel so sad for my younger self. I let another person verbally knock me down and take my power from me, simply because they were in a more senior position than I was. I subsequently changed what I wore to be accepted and fit in better at work.

We often give away our power to stay safe. To stay in our comfort zone, and not make waves. It is less risky for sure. The problem is it also holds us back. We relinquish our ability to have our voice heard and be seen as our authentic selves. In the masculine model, power creates competition and a sense of scarcity, as if only a few chosen ones can be powerful. This is based on the belief that there must be winners and losers. As a result, power can be abused to control others. It can be used to invoke fear and keep others in their place and playing small. There are certainly many examples of that in the daily newspapers and history books.

The masculine model of power, which has been the dominant power model for millennia, is based on the concepts of scarcity and fear. It is a construct where assertiveness and competition are used to gain power. That model had never been my mental model of the world, nor what felt more genuine and authentic to me as a person and a leader. I had always felt more comfortable being collaborative, caring, and inclusive as a leader. I believed in abundance and that all of us have gifts to contribute. That was how I approached working with my teams.

I finally recognized, after much reflection, that I identified more with a feminine construct of power. The feminine model focuses on nurturing and empathy, cooperation, and collaboration.

It is relationship-based and being receptive to others. One model is not better than another, and the most skilled leaders will try to balance their masculine and feminine traits and energies. That said, the organizations I worked for were all very hierarchical, and the masculine construct was the primary one in play. Used equally by male and female leaders. For a woman, that was tricky to navigate. If I was too assertive or direct, I could be labeled as difficult or a bitch. If I were empathetic and caring, I would be seen as too "soft" and unable to make tough decisions. The problem was not a new one. Women collectively have been struggling with that for millennia. If you were not accepted and gained the approval of those in power, you could be left to starve or to die. We had to keep quiet, do what we were asked to do and play small. Our rocking the boat could have negative consequences.

The awareness that the archaic masculine model of power was not aligned with my authentic self was a game changer for me. I began to stepping into my personal power and letting go of the need for external recognition. I started to feel more confident in my decision making and in sharing my ideas. I began to speak with my authentic voice. I began to sit at the conference room table like I owned it, and completely deserved to be there. And I was seen by others as belonging there as well.

I gained confidence, got a business degree, and changed jobs. I chose an organization whose values were more aligned with my own, and which chose me for the skills and talents I could bring to them. I could embrace my personal power and become even more successful and much happier. I was much more "me" as a leader and team member. I began to wear bright colors to work and shoes with bling. I felt more empowered and felt more comfortable using my voice. Even when it was not what my boss or leadership wanted to hear. Looking back, I wish I had learned to step into and own my personal power much earlier in my career.

I have seen this process work for my clients as well. One example that stands out for me is a woman I will call Molly. Molly was a working mom with several children and a husband who was controlling and verbally abusive. Molly worked long hours. She always looked exhausted and unhappy, and suffered from chronic headaches. She was dissatisfied with her marriage but did not see a way out for herself. She had given away her power to her husband, who often treated her more like a child than a partner. She felt stuck.

Working with Molly, she discovered how misaligned her values were with her husband's and that she needed to change her personal narrative for herself. She wanted to regain her power and have more control of her life. She made significant changes in her relationship and in her job. She was able to align her work and life with her values and purpose, and step into a new, more meaningful role at work. The outcome was amazing to witness. She was happy, smiling, full of self-confidence and hope. The last time I saw her, she was pleased with her life and her relationship with her children and expressed compassion for her partner. She also realized and accepted her accountability and responsibility for how she had previously given her power away.

Personal power is available to everyone. We all deserve to own our power and use it for good. We all deserve to share our gifts and shine our light. To speak our voice and contribute our best to make the world a better place. So how does one learn to step into their personal power and really own it? First, you need to recognize if you are giving your power away. If so, you will feel frustrated, disrespected, or not heard. You will not think that you are recognized for your accomplishments. You may start to lose confidence in yourself. Awareness of those emotions and thoughts, and how they feel or are expressed physically in your body, is the first step. As an example, I had a client who felt they were not being valued and respected at work. They thought their manager did not trust them, and in fact, was holding back the individual back from being creative and innovative in their role.

This individual realized that they had been giving their power to their manager, and once aware of this fact, they could do something to change it. They decided to connect with a peer and develop a better way to document their work caring for patients. The ability to work with a peer and create a more efficient and easier to use document made them feel excited and more empowered. They realized they could be a leader in their role regardless of their job title or how their manager was behaving. That self-discovery and growth made a massive difference in that client's self-confidence and feeling of self-worth. You have the ability to make this happen in your life as well. Once you become aware that you have ceded your power, and more conscious of the feelings that you create for yourself, then you can consciously plan to change. You can take the time to reflect on who you have a tendency to give your power to, and mentally thank them for helping you be more discerning of the response this creates for you. Yes, intentionally thank them. The misalignment of what you want vs. those sensations and sense of frustration is helping you to grow and more fully develop into your most authentic and powerful self.

Once you have become more mindful and conscious of your behavior, plan to incorporate small changes in your actions and habits. List out your strengths and areas of opportunity, or update your resume. Get to know yourself better by writing down your thoughts and ideas. Be more willing to be vulnerable and honest with others by sharing your feedback and opinions in a caring and respectful way. Wear different clothes or add new colors to your repertoire. Change your hairstyle or decorate your cubicle or office to better reflect your individual personality. Be open to embracing the concept of abundance, with the belief that there is plenty of power and success to go around for all. Be willing to speak your voice with grace and sincerity.

Not everyone will be happy with what you have to say or will agree with it. It may not change the decisions that are made in your organization. It may not change another person's behavior. That is perfectly alright. If you speak with your true voice and are your authentic self, you retain your personal power, and others will begin to recognize and acknowledge it. As you institute these small changes you will build your self-confidence and self-esteem and self-acceptance. How cool is that! And, if the current masculine construct of power does not feel right to you, that is okay too. You can embrace a more feminine model and work in that construct instead. Whatever feels most authentic and "right" to you. You may need to consider a change, such as who you work for, your role or your location. That is all part of the gift of growing as a person and professional. The gift of getting to know yourself deeply and also what matters most to you, and to learn not to compromise to "fit in." To own your power and bring your best self to the world every day.

# Chapter 5
# POWER POINTS

- You have the power to rewrite your story and replace it with one that is more aligned with your adult, authentic self.
- People often give their power to others to be accepted, stay safe and not make waves.
- The masculine power construct is one based on fear and scarcity. This results in winners and losers and can lead to abuse of power.
- Becoming self-aware of when and to whom you give your power away allows you to consciously plan regain your personal power.
- You have the ability to decide what you want to unlearn, and which outdated and limiting beliefs you want or need to replace as you move forward.
- The repeated use of positive affirmations, body gestures, or postures will allow for new pathways and neuronal connections to become more easily traveled. As that happens, your emotions and physiological responses will be captured in your subconscious memory banks.

# SECTION THREE

# RISE AND SHINE

*"Even if you are on the right track, you'll get runover if you just sit there."*
Will Rogers

# CHAPTER 6

# UNLOCK

## Bring to light your highest potential

*"To dare is to lose one's footing momentarily.*
*To not dare is to lose oneself."*
*Soren Kierkegaard*

*"Intentionally leaving the comfort zone goes*
*hand-in-hand with developing a growth*
*mindset. While the fixed mindset keeps*
*us trapped by fear of failure, the growth*
*mindset expands the possible. It inspires us*
*to learn and take healthy risks, leading to*
*positive outcomes across life domains."*
*Oliver Page*

YOU HAVE DONE TREMENDOUS WORK. YOU HAVE IDENTIFIED YOUR reason for being, passions, and vision for the future. You have successfully exposed your limiting beliefs and outmoded ways of perceiving yourself and have begun the process of replacing them. Now, it is time to unlock your true potential. The definition of unlock, is "to be free from restraints and restrictions." We often place ourselves in self-imposed chains that bind us and keep us from reaching our highest potential. Unconsciously chosen shackles that immobilize us and keep us from achieving our goals and personal best. Have you ever considered what you are truly capable of? Have you ever shined a light on all your possibilities and potential? Most likely, you have not. And if you have, I celebrate and commend you! You are in the minority.

You do have the power to unlock your destiny, and to free yourself from the chains that you have unknowingly bound yourself with. Those that grew out of playing it safe, playing small, and staying under the radar. The bonds of not feeling worthy enough, good enough, or from the fear of facing a challenge or some form of rejection. You can be free of those self-inflicted chains and be your most powerful, strong, and best self. However, it means pushing yourself out of what is comfortable for you. It requires you to be a bit daring, a bit bold, and to have some faith. Yes, you will have to get out of your comfort zone.

If you are like most people, playing outside of your comfort zone can be scary. When I was fifty years old, I signed up for my first Tough Mudder, an endurance obstacle course. I had no idea what I was getting myself into, as I was unfamiliar with the challenging event. However, my team was signing up for it and as their leader I thought I should give it a try as well. I was hoping to help build trust and camaraderie with my team members. I figured I was in pretty good physical shape and did a lot of walking and jogging, so how hard could it be? After I signed up, I did some research and quickly came to the realization that this event was more than I had bargained for. A Tough Mudder is a ten- to twelve-mile-long muddy course with an extreme set of obstacles to overcome along the way. It is an endurance race that was created by William Dean, who founded the Tough Mudder. You run, crawl and swim in mud. A whole lot of mud.

The mud did not phase me too much, nor did the length of the course. I had participated in 5k events in the past and was used to walking and jogging up to four or five miles at a time. My team was excited that I was going to join them. We planned our matching outfits and what time to meet on the day of the event. One of the team members had participated before and she shared her best tips with us to help us prepare. As the race day drew near, we had the opportunity to see what our obstacles would be, and they were daunting. Especially the last one for newbies to the race, such as myself. After trekking ten miles or so in the mud and scaling high walls, swimming in mud and carrying a teammate on my back for fifty yards (okay, it may have been ten yards, but it sure felt like fifty), I was going to have to crawl under and over chicken wire in a pool of mud that contained electrical shocks. Basically, forcing myself to get shocked at least once to make it through successfully to the end of the course. I started to feel a little intimidated by the thought of those formidable obstacles, but I knew I could not back out and disappoint my team.

I was feeling very much out of my comfort zone by the day of the race. As I drove to the event, I began to question my choice to participate. That was until I saw my team as they prepped for the upcoming endurance race. They were excited that I was with them and we cheered each other on as we gathered for the start of the race. I stepped out of my comfort zone and onto the obstacle course. It was tiring, long, grimy, and grueling. It forced me to try things I had never physically done before. I had to rely on others to overcome many of the obstacles and had to do the same for others who were behind me. The team did a fantastic job supporting each other emotionally, mentally and physically. I did not successfully complete every obstacle, but I tried everyone. And finally, I was at the last obstacle. The muddy electrical shock field was filled with chicken wire at varying heights. My last hurdle. I was paralyzed by the thought of what was coming. I also knew this was my final obstacle.

I watched as several of my teammates moved through the mud and cried out with the discomfort and surprise of the shocks. I understood that the shocks were not life-threatening, just a nuisance. Still the idea made me very uncomfortable. Feeling a little more confident having made it that far through the course, I moved slowly into the muddy field of chicken wire. I was now several miles outside of my comfort zone and getting zapped more than I had anticipated. I made it to the end, after more than a few electrical shocks. I just stood a moment, to catch my breath. It had been hours of physical and emotional stress, and I had finished the course.

As I walked off the course, I began to feel elated. I had done it! I had been way outside of my comfort zone and pushed myself to stay on the course and complete the race. I recognized that I was stronger and more resilient than I had thought I was. Once back home I reflected on the experience. I had not enjoyed being out of my comfort zone. It had been unnerving. I had been afraid of the obstacles, of being unable to finish, and of getting physically injured. It had been a lesson for me in the importance of teamwork, humility, and the willingness to take risks. I soon made the connection between that very physical challenge with the more emotional and mental challenges that come with being a leader, manager, and parent. Let's face it, it is not a natural inclination to hurl oneself into danger or push past emotional, physical, or mental obstacles. And yet, to do just that can be such an opportunity to grow and learn. A chance to realize you are stronger than you know. To show yourself that you are more resilient than you give yourself credit for. An opportunity to build confidence in yourself.

I signed up for the same endurance race the following year and brought along my daughter to experience it for herself. She was more physically fit than me, much younger, and able to overcome obstacles easily. This time around, I knew better what to expect and felt more mentally ready. I could not complete all the challenges, but made it to the finish line a little after my daughter. It was still an uncomfortable experience, but I had confidence that all would be okay. And it was. Well, more than okay, it was a blast! I would have never thought I would enjoy being pushed past my limits and a muddy mess, yet there I was. Smiling and hugging my daughter, knowing she had forced herself out of her comfort zone and had grown as well. I have had the privilege of working with others to help them to move past their comfort zone in order to grow and learn. For example, a woman who made the decision to leave the organization she had been a part of for many years to embrace a senior leadership role in another company. She has grown immensely in her leadership capabilities and self-confidence, and is bringing much value to her new role. She is also happier and smiles a lot more.

Another client decided to apply for a director level position in her organization, despite being a manager for a short time, and being much younger than many of the team members who would be reporting to her. She pushed herself out of her comfort level and interviewed for the position. She was thrilled to get the promotion and thankful she had taken the opportunity to apply for the role despite her fear of not being "good enough" and needing to be vulnerable and open with the rest of the department. The process further developed her level of self-esteem and made her feel more empowered in her workplace.

The whole concept of comfort zone and pushing past fear to learn and grow is not a new one. Pushing past the comfort zone requires one to push past their fear. That is not an easy thing to do, and not a natural response to stress. The term has been around for decades and became popular in the 1990's based on the work of Judith Bardwick, *Danger in the Comfort Zone* (Amazon books, 1991). Research has confirmed that behavioral studies conducted at the turn of the twentieth century identified that mice would respond negatively when running in a maze and receiving electrical shocks. They would hide rather than complete the maze for their reward. Similar responses were noted in human subjects when placed into more anxiety-producing situations; they would perform worse than if introduced to a more acceptable level of fear and anxiety (Yerkes-Dodson law, 1907). I can totally understand the change in behavior, as I certainly felt anxiety facing electric shocks at the end of the Tough Mudder. Trust me, I did not perform at my highest level with that obstacle!

If you think back to Maslow's Hierarchy of Needs in Chapter 3, you need to reach self-actualization to get to your highest potential.

To achieve that you must push out of your comfort zone and face your fears, and be open to failure. That allows you to move into the learning and growth zones, as noted in the image below from the Positive Psychology.com Toolkit.

## Figure 4: Leaving the Comfort Zone

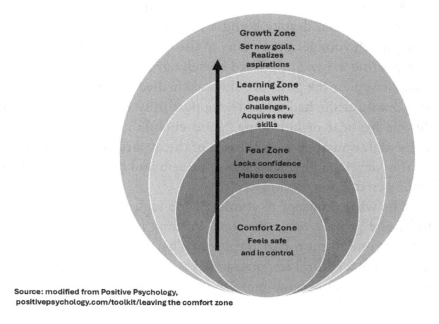

Source: modified from Positive Psychology, positivepsychology.com/toolkit/leaving the comfort zone

Comfort zones can vary depending on the situation and personal experience. You may feel very comfortable pushing yourself out of your comfort zone in a physical challenge, such as an endurance obstacle course, but have difficulty moving past your comfort zone when faced with a leadership challenge. For example, an unexpected request to take the lead on a project or present to the Board of Directors with almost no notice due to a colleague's illness. Understanding where you tend to shy away from straying out of your comfort zone can be very helpful. It can highlight the areas you must focus on to reach your greatest potential. On the flip side, identifying the places where you feel more comfortable pushing past your fears and previous examples of success in doing so can help you be aware of the best place to start to gain confidence in yourself. You can use your past successes and continue to foster your self-confidence in that topic area by continued challenges in that subject.

Let's say, you are successful in completing a five-mile run, and then a half marathon. You can continue to focus on building your ability and self-confidence to complete a marathon as your next goal. Once you can trust the process, you can apply challenging yourself in an area you feel less confident in.

To unlock your highest potential, you need to get into the learning and growth zones noted above. How to achieve this? By building on your prior success of moving out of your comfort zone. Think back and reflect on where you have been able to face your fears and achieve a new skill or complete a personal or professional challenge. You can use that previous accomplishment as a starting point. You know you can do this and be successful because you have done it before. You can use that sense of confidence and knowledge that you have faced your challenges head-on and moved past them to grow and flourish. Build on that foundation of success to try a new challenge or create a new goal for yourself.

You can use rapid, small cycles of challenges or change to help you build more trust in yourself and your abilities. Successive cycles of challenge or change will create momentum for you, and help you progress to a higher level of self-esteem and self-assurance. The concept of using rapid small cycles of change has been shown to be a highly effective model for performance and process improvement in many industries. It is a tried-and-true method that was developed by W. Edward Demmings (1943, 1957), and has been used for decades, including in health care. In health care this approach has been widely adopted to improve safety and quality for patients, health care providers, and their care teams. The cycle of change is often referred to as the PDSA cycle; Plan, Do, Study, Act. This is founded on the theory that not every change results in an improvement, so each cycle of change should be assessed for its results, and the approach can be modified to get closer to the desired outcome or result. The Institute for Healthcare Improvement calls this method the Model for Improvement.

### Figure 5: Cycle of Change

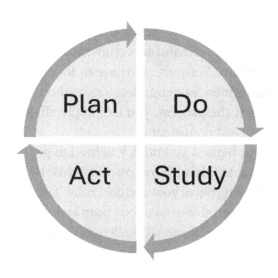

By instituting small changes and assessing them to adapt and achieve a higher level of performance, you can falter and learn, and then continue to move forward towards your goal. The model allows you to take small steps and build confidence over time, as you move to higher and higher levels of performance or accomplishments. This approach can be used is an individual and an organizational setting, like a health system or hospital. The momentum is created as you complete each small test or challenge and reflect on what worked and what could have been better. Then, make a modification and give it another try. This helps to reduce the fear of failure, because the approach is about trying your best and keeping a growth mindset. Each small challenge provides you with information or data, to help you adjust for the next round and improve your outcomes. The key is to stay open to learning and growing rather than winning or losing. In the POWER UP framework, the phases of each cycle include to setting an aspiration, challenging yourself, assessing how the challenge went, and then to editing or adjusting for the next cycle

The process begins with first being very clear about what you want to achieve, by defining your goal(s). For example, to run a half marathon. That is terrific, but what if you haven't been a runner in the past? You like to go for long walks and occasionally jog for a bit. No problem. You analyze the challenge and realize it will take a series of cycles to learn what works for you. You then can assess what needs to be modified or adjusted for the next round. Your goal statement should be very simple and action-oriented. The best practice is to ensure it is a SMART goal. A SMART goal is one that is Specific, Measurable, Achievable, Relevant and Time-bound. Here is an example below:

> *Goal: Run a half marathon within the next six months.*
> *Challenge One: Complete a one mile run within 10 days.*
> *Measure of Success: Complete one mile and run the entire mile.*

Terrific! Now, you have a small test for yourself and a timeframe to complete it in! You give it a go and realize that you can only run half that distance and then need to walk for a bit. Awesome job! You just succeeded at doing more than you could in the past and you can continue to build on that success moving forward.

"Okay, but I didn't get to my goal." That is technically correct. However, you did your best and were able to run a half a mile straight. Go you! It's time to try another round and make a correction where it is needed. You may recognize that a slower pace will help you to run the whole mile straight. You do the test of change and run that entire mile without stopping or walking. You successfully completed your first challenge and can now develop another challenge to get you closer to your final goal. All the while you are learning, with each cycle. You are building confidence, gaining knowledge and pushing yourself towards your goal.

This process can work for any type of goal you set for yourself. For example, I had a patient who wanted to control her blood sugars better. She had poorly controlled diabetes and knew she needed to make a change. Her goal was to not eat marshmallow fluff and peanut butter sandwiches in the middle of the night and to make a better snack choice within a certain time frame. Now, you may ask yourself if that is really a SMART goal. It might not be a goal for you but it was something she felt she could control and build confidence and trust in herself. She was able to switch to snacking on low-calorie popcorn instead and began walking up and down her driveway several times a day. By checking her blood sugar frequently, she learned that walking helped to lower it, along with the change to popcorn versus a sugary sandwich at night. Her sugars gradually became better controlled, and she continued to make adjustments in her behaviors and lifestyle. She was thrilled by her achievements and even became a peer mentor for other diabetic patients in the clinic.

The process of using small cycles of change to build momentum and move you closer to your goals can be likened to a flywheel. As it begins to move forward the momentum builds, and the performance improves and propels you forward to reach your ultimate goal. Using this type of framework also allows you to look back at the successive cycles of change and appreciate not only reaching a goal, but also your ability to move out of your comfort zone to learn and grow.

**Figure 6: POWER UP Flywheel**

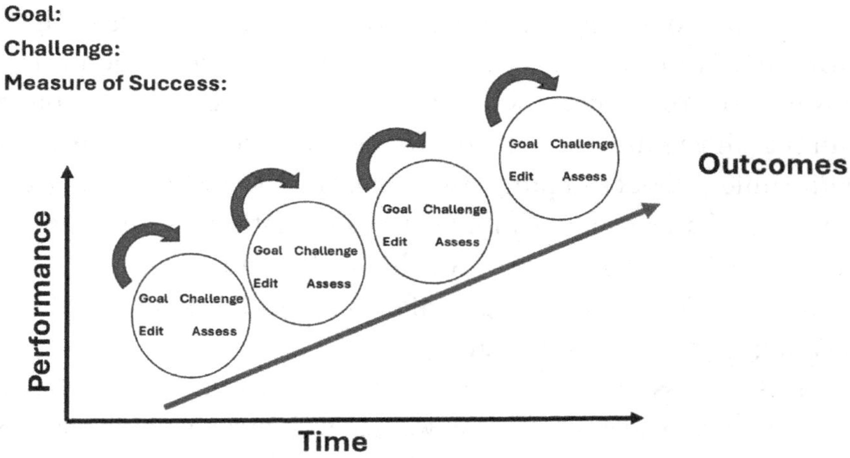
Goal:
Challenge:
Measure of Success:
Goal Challenge
Edit Assess
Goal Challenge
Edit Assess
Goal Challenge
Edit Assess
Goal Challenge
Edit Assess
Outcomes
Performance
Time

You may think, "That would work for a physical challenge, but what about a professional one?" It works the same way. What if the goal is moving to a new managerial role at work? An opening for a manager role has just become available in your department. You have not been a manager in the past, and you know you have the required skills and knowledge in your area of expertise. Well, you have defined the goal and can begin to develop challenges for yourself. Perhaps, you could out to the recruiter or your boss to learn more about the role and to share your interest in the position as the first "test." The thought of this may make you feel queasy, uncomfortable, and even scared. That is a good sign. It means you have identified that this will require you to move out of your comfort zone. "Wait, what if I am not good enough? What if they find out (fill in the blank with your specific fear, and yes, we all have them)."

If this test feels like too much, you can adjust the test to something less risky for you. For example, update your resume and highlight the skills, knowledge, and experiences you have that make you a strong candidate for the new role. Once that is completed, not only do you have a great resume to share with your current boss, but you have also captured all the current value you bring to your organization. You have documented your talents, abilities, and strengths. The action of updating your resume helps to build your self-confidence and it feels pretty good to celebrate your accomplishments and knowledge! Perhaps at this point you can return to the first challenge of reaching out to your boss and the recruiter about your interest in the role. You have an updated resume, a clear sense of the value you bring to your organization, and a newfound sense of self-esteem.

When engaged in this work your self-doubts and insecurities may pop up from time to time. Negative self-talk may creep in. Those feelings of not feeling good enough, of imposter syndrome, and fear of failing. That is okay, because when you are aware of those thoughts you can stop them in their tracks and remind yourself that you are simply doing a small test or challenge. You can tell yourself that this process is all about learning and growing, so there is no failure. Simply use this data for your next small test or challenge, nothing more. By framing the process with a more positive, growth mindset, the fears and self-doubt can be replaced with a sense of self-confidence, self-assurance, and anticipation. Yes, anticipation! Replace any fears or sinking feeling in your gut with a sense of excitement and anticipation. With a little nervous excitement and a sense of personal power. You know you can do this. You have succeeded before with a different type of challenge, and you know that you can be successful again. Remember, any small step forward is progress. Those small steps build momentum for you and move you closer to your ultimate goal. Do not forget to celebrate the small wins along the way. You are learning and growing. Before you know it, you will achieve your target!

# Chapter 6
# POWER POINTS

- You have the power to unlock and bring to light your highest potential.
- To reach your highest potential, you need to have a growth mindset and be open to learning and growing.
- Moving out of your comfort zone and into learning and growth zones is vital to in unlocking your highest potential.
- Pushing out of your comfort zone will make you feel awkward or uneasy, which is normal. That is part of the process.
- Use past experiences of pushing out of your comfort zone and were successful demonstrating to yourself that you can achieve a new goal as well!
- Small, rapid cycles of challenges can help you to build confidence and momentum towards your goal.
- A SMART goal is best to use; Smart, Measurable, Achievable, Relevant, and Time-bound.

# CHAPTER 7

# POSSIBILITY

## Cultivate a possibility mindset

*In this moment, there is plenty of time. In this moment, you are*
*precisely as you should be. In this moment, there is infinite possibility.*
Victoria Moran

POSSIBILITY THINKING IS HAVING A MINDSET THAT IS OPEN TO growth and acknowledges that there are unlimited possibilities available. It allows one to be creative and use their imagination to design new ways to solve problems and achieve their goals. It also fosters a sense of abundance. A belief that there is more than enough success, wealth, and opportunity for all. With this positive mindset, barriers are just bumps you encounter while navigating the road. There are no limits to what can be accomplished. Only infinite opportunities that one can take advantage of, learn from, and utilize to manifest their best, most authentic self.

You have worked hard to clarify your values and passions and rediscover your purpose and reason for being. You have exposed the outdated and limiting beliefs that resulted in negative self-talk and have influenced your decisions. You have taken action and have replaced them with a more positive and aligned lens to view and experience yourself and the world. You have unlocked your true potential by challenging yourself to face your fears and push into your learning and growth zones. Without judgment, only a willingness for personal development and highest potential. Now it is time for you to unleash your imagination and create your future possibilities.

Life will always hand us disruptions. Problems can crop up at any time. For example, the car won't start the day you have an important meeting to get to (oops, forgot to get the annual car maintenance done). Or your middle schooler notifies you at 7 AM that they need a grab bag gift and a snack to contribute today at school, and you are already running behind. Maybe you forgot your wallet and are already through the checkout lane at the grocery store, or your boss requests a meeting with you this afternoon and informs you that they are eliminating your job with only a few weeks' notice. All these scenarios can be challenging and a bit difficult to deal with. However, you have the power to choose your reaction to those situations. You can get upset and fret over the annoyances, or you can be open to new opportunities and the possibility for creative solutions. It is all in how you view the issues. One of my favorite books is *The Art of Possibility*, by Ben and Rosamund Zanders. It starts out with a story about two shoe salespeople who go to another country to sell shoes. One salesperson sends a note back to the home office that there is no opportunity as none of the people he meets wear shoes. The other person sends a note exclaiming how wonderful it is to be a shoe salesperson because none of the people he is meeting wear shoes. Both salespeople had the same experience, however they responded to the circumstance very differently. The one who saw potential viewed the situation with a mindset of abundance and possibility.

You have infinite possibilities open to you. All you need to do is define what it is you want to manifest. What it is that you want to accomplish, feel, or be. It is totally up to you; if you think it, you can do it. You can design your future, and your possibilities. For example, I wanted to write this book and become an author. I had no experience as an author, other than drafting white papers and research grant applications over the years. So why did I think I could become an author and have a book published?

Because I saw it as a possibility for myself.

I decided that if others could write books and be published authors, I could be as well. If not me, then who? Who else had my unique perspective and wisdom to share with others.? No one. That is when I decided to forge ahead and write this book.

I connected with a literary agent and sent along a few book proposals, which did not get me very far. However, I did learn how to create a book proposal and how the publishing world works. I received constructive feedback that helped me improve my writing skills. I found a self-publishing option to work with, and learned how the book market is navigated. I researched book genres, how launch a book and wrote my less than awesome first draft. The result, I made it possible for myself to become an author. I found solutions for my barriers and bumps along the road. I learned a tremendous amount of new knowledge, and I became more confident in myself. This helped me to be more self-assured in launching a new business, writing a blog, and expanding my options for future possibilities. You can do this as well.

Start with your unique purpose and vision statement for yourself. In Chapter One, you rediscovered your authentic self and reason for being. You described what lights you up inside, and your superpowers to share with the world. Now it is time to apply possibility thinking to your deepest desires and dreams.

Write down your purpose/mission and your vision statement. Use the information you described and documented based on the exercises and prompts in Chapter One, and your vision statement. Brainstorm at least ten different possibilities for your future below. The sky is the limit here. Actually, your options are limitless! Do not let negative self-talk creep into your head while you do this exercise. In this space dare to dream as big and as boldly as you can. Here, money is no object, and there are no roadblocks to your dreams and desires. Just space for you to be open to all potential options.

Unsure how to brainstorm? Write down on a whiteboard, a piece of paper or your favorite device anything that pops into your mind as a possibility, based on your values, passions, superpowers, skills, and vision for yourself. Passionate about old cars and an expert at organization and project management? Have a vision to be an entrepreneur? Go for it! Write them all down.

Think BIG. Your brainstorm may include opening your own muscle car restoration company, creating a Facebook neighborhood for vintage car sales, or securing a new position with Mecum to oversee and manage their annual car shows and expand them internationally. Say baking is your forte, and you have a degree in art illustration. You also have a personal vision to travel across Europe. Your brainstorming list may include taking a pastry course in Paris for the summer, the use of art illustrations to create a new type of decorative cake or to get a job on a river cruise boat line in Europe as their pastry chef. While you are at it, add writing a cookbook that teaches others to use your art illustration techniques to create edible works of art. Or perhaps, launch a social media cooking channel and star as the chef in your own baking show. Maybe you add winning the British Spring Baking Championship in three years.

But wait, isn't brainstorming a group activity? Yes, it is often done as a group activity, and can it also be very effectively done as an individual. In fact, there have been studies that show individual brainstorming can be better in certain situations. If the problem is a very complex one, a group can sometimes generate fewer ideas than if done alone. More moderately complex issues are solved better in a group brainstorming session. You have most likely been in a group setting where your ideas are shot down quickly as the others are voicing their ideas. This can inhibit creative idea generation. This prompt is for you to think about all possibilities, and is a more complex situation, which lends itself well to individual brainstorming.

During this process it can be useful to do multiple rounds and think of as many possibilities as you can. Focus on "what" may be a possibility for you, and do not worry about the "how." The things you list may seem improbable right now, but that does not mean it is not a possibility for you. You need to suspend all judgment and

76

self-criticism during this process. That is right, no judging. If you can dream it and think about it, it is a possibility!

Once your brainstorming session is complete, review the list and refine your options. You can place them into key categories or rank them by preference. You can prioritize them based on your reason for being and personal statement developed in Chapter One. You can also look to see what dependencies your ideas have. That can sometimes help you better clarify the ideas and identify a natural sequence of possibilities. For example, you identified five possibilities for yourself including becoming a plastic surgeon, opening a Medi spa, and getting a certification as an aesthetician. You also listed traveling to Indonesia to learn about natural botanicals for use in skin care products and working for an established dermatology clinic as a chemist in the botanical skin care industry. Becoming a plastic surgeon takes many years of education, surgical residency, and a fellowship in plastic surgery. You may decide to train as an aesthetician first to help pay your medical school bills. Or perhaps you will decide a chemistry degree is the best first step for you to make your possibilities become real.

In this example, you concluded that completing a certificate program and getting a job as an aesthetician was the option that made the most sense for you as a start. You also discovered a fantastic botanical retreat in Indonesia that features natural skin care products. By applying possibility thinking you brainstormed and were open to new possibilities for yourself. If you had not created that innovative list, you may never had noticed the retreat invitation pop up in your daily social media feed.

Terrific job! You have withheld being Judge Judgy and stopped the negative self-talk in your head. You have developed a bodacious list of possibilities for yourself. Ones that align with your highest motivations, purpose and vision for your future. Ones that may seem outrageous, a bit crazy and even make you laugh or giggle. If that happens you are on to something. In fact, humor is directly connected to a higher level of creativity. Paul Plsek, an international expert in creativity and innovation, believes that if you laugh at an idea, it is a positive indication that the idea is a good one. It may be an innovative and even ingenious idea. That is possibility thinking at its best. In fact, research has shown laughter to be highly beneficial in the creative thinking process. Humor and laughing stimulates areas in the brain linked to problem-solving and idea generation. It also supports the synthesis or blending of information to help you develop more unanticipated ideas. How cool is that! Be sure to approach this exercise with a growth mindset. One filled with the notion of abundance, limitless possibility, and humor.

Now, let's go back to what you brainstormed in response to the prompt above. Once your list of possibilities is complete, and you have refined the ideas, make sure to identify any dependencies in them. Does one have to happen before another one can be achieved? Next, rank them by priority or try sequencing them. Then, it is time to begin manifesting your possibilities. Pick the one that seems to be most aligned with your vision for yourself and which you feel most drawn to. It may be the one that made you laugh so hard, it brought you to tears, or surprised you when you heard yourself giggling. It may be the one you are most curious about, or makes you feel really excited about making it a reality. Once you have the first possibility picked out it is time to move to manifesting.

What is manifesting? Manifesting is the act of identifying what you want to bring into your reality. Into your life. It is letting the universe know what your intention is for yourself. It is about bringing into your current life what you wish for. Manifesting is a bit like magic. You dream it and then decide that it will happen. How it happens may not be clear. The how does not matter at this point, only that you will it to be. And you not only will it to be, but you also clearly visualize it. You take that possibility, place yourself in the future, and describe what it would feel like to achieve your desire or wish even before it becomes a reality for you.

The what is your heart's desire, your top possibility. You don't have to know the how, you just need to trust in the process. Much like you were asked to hold judgement with the possibility thinking brainstorming process. You are asked to trust that the "how" will find its way to you. If you are conscious of what it is you want to have as a reality for yourself, your brain will look for a way to make it real. Your subconscious mind will be on the lookout, canvasing all the data it takes in to help you. Its job is to make that thought into a reality for you. It cannot happen by itself though. You must act. You must immerse yourself in the future possibility you dreamed of. You need to fully describe it. You need to feel and visualize what having your possibility would feel and look like. That is correct, you must feel it and be clear of what success looks like once it is accomplished. Place yourself in the future as if the possibility has already been achieved.

How would you know that you had achieved your possibility? Use your five senses and words to describe what having your possibility in place would mean for you. The more descriptive the better. Write it down, draw a picture, or say it aloud. Better yet, share it with a friend or family member. What that apartment would look and smell like. What that money in the bank would allow you to do. What your book signing tour for your decorative baking cookbook would be like. Or, how having the first customer walk into your new mechanic shop for restoration of their 1963, split back window corvette makes you burst with excitement and pride. A vision board can help bring that possibility to life for you. A vision board is a way for you to create a physical portrayal of what it is that you desire to achieve. It can be made up of words, symbols, colors, or pictures. The goal is to help make your dream something tangible for you to use as a way of visualizing your goals. Whatever method works best for you, immerse yourself in that future state. That way your brain knows what it is it should be on the lookout for in order to help you make the dream or idea a reality. It will scout for the opportunities to support you in achieving your future set of possibilities. As opportunities appear you will need to continue to act on them to get closer to that future desired state. For example, the friend who shares that there is an unexpected opening in a two-week long pastry class in Paris next month, and do you know anyone who may want to attend? Yes, you do, it is you! Act on the unexpected opportunity and apply. Who knows what might come of the experience? Or you attend a

Mecum car auction and notice a flyer with a job opening listed. They are looking for an expert in muscle cars. Apply! Your brain just helped you notice the job opportunity for a reason. It was scouting all the data in your surroundings for something that aligned with or supported your future possibilities. It may lead to a bigger role in their enterprise, even the one you dreamed of for yourself. The universe holds an endless number of opportunities for you. Adopt a possibility mindset, stay open, and be curious as you create the future you desire. The only limits are the ones you impose on yourself.

## Chapter 7
## POWER POINTS

- A possibility mindset is one that is open to growth and acknowledges that there are unlimited possibilities.
- Possibility thinking allows one to be creative and use their imagination to design new ways to solve problems and achieve their goals.
- Embrace abundance. There is more than enough success, wealth, and happiness for all.
- Individual brainstorming can be effective and enhance the process of idea generation for more complex situations, like defining limitless possibilities for your future.
- Humor and creative thinking are directly related. If you laugh at an idea that you created while brainstorming, that means you are on to something spectacular!
- Laughing stimulates creativity and problem-solving areas within the brain.
- When you are clear on what you want for your future, use the power of manifesting. It will help your subconscious mind scout for opportunities so that you can take action.
- Action is key in manifesting and achieving your goals. When an opportunity presents itself, act and move forward with trust and self-confidence.

# CHAPTER 8

## CONCLUSION

You have successfully worked through the POWER UP framework and have rediscovered your authentic self. Using the exercises and prompts throughout the book has allowed you to better understand how and why you have made the decisions in your life that have brought you to your current reality. The work may have been uncomfortable for you at times, which is a positive thing. That means that you have pushed out of your comfort zone and into learning and growth zones to build and strengthen your self-awareness. And your understanding of how you got to the present place in your life. You have more awareness of your negative self-talk, your limiting beliefs and outdated ways of seeing yourself and experiencing the world. Now you can consciously decide if you need or want to change anything. You have the power to unlearn something that does not fit or align with your current self or future vision for yourself and replace it with something new. A fresh way of seeing yourself, thinking about yourself, or narrative of who you truly are. You must be intentional with what you want to let go of and what you want to create for your future self. Then you must practice it and repeat what you want to replace the old, outdated things with. Use positive affirmations and stop any negative self-talk as it becomes present in your consciousness. Anchor your new

81

positive self-talk and vision with physical gestures, postures, and your voice. Describe it in writing, through the use of a picture, or the creation of a vision board.

You are the captain of your brain, and your conscious thoughts and their directions to your subconscious mind can be very powerful. Practice manifesting and see yourself in the future place you have envisioned. Fully describe what it will look, feel, and smell like.. Use all your senses to bring that future state into your present consciousness. You have learned tools and techniques to challenge yourself and move out of your comfort zone to learn and grow. A growth mindset and openness to learning and developing will allow you to make small cycles of change and adjust as you go to achieve the aspirations you set for yourself. This will help you to build confidence and gain more trust in your capabilities. Go for it, and unlock your highest potential. There is so much you have to offer the world. By adopting an approach to life that is based on possibility, you know that you can achieve your goals. If you can think it, it can be a reality. Don't play small, think big and boldly. The world needs all your possibilities. It needs you to shine your light and share your unique skills and talents. It needs you to become your best authentic self.

To review, the POWER UP framework is described below:

Pause, Take time to reflect and rediscover who you are
Observe, Be aware of your choices and current reality
Wonder, Discover how you got here
Expose, Become conscious of your limiting beliefs
Replace, You have the power to rewrite your story
Unlock, Bring to light your highest potential
Possibility, Cultivate a possibility mindset

You can return to any of the exercises in the book that you need to keep building your self-confidence and to develop yourself further. Any individual chapter and set of prompts can be used along your journey to help you grow and continue to build your self-awareness.

Your ability to create new neural pathways in your brain to support the changes you want to make. Changes in how you experience the world and yourself, or changes in your actions and behaviors. You have the power to create the life you most desire. You have the power to transform and become your best authentic self.

# AFTERWORD

# Glowing Forward

*"Simply shine your light on the road ahead, and you are helping others to see their way out of darkness."*
Katrina Mayer

You are a unique and divine being. No one else in the world has your skills, talents, perspectives, and passions. You are needed in this world right now to shine your light and share your gifts. Holding back and playing small does not help you or anyone else. It certainly does not honor all that you have to give to the world and all that you are. I believe that if you shine your light, you also enable others to shine. As a collective, we can make the world a better place. We can help to preserve and sustain our planet. We can be of service to others and share our gifts to enhance our collective experience, happiness, and joy.

The POWER UP framework was developed with that concept in mind. To help others reflect and rediscover their North star, values, purpose, and superpowers. To enable people to recognize their limited and outdated ways of experiencing the world and themselves, and to stay curious about where and when these beliefs were formed. To teach others how to replace those limiting beliefs with ones that are more aligned with their authentic adult selves. To step into their power and truly own it. To let go of what does not serve them in their life and embrace their highest potential. To move towards the future with a mindset of possibility and abundance.

The process that the book provides for you can help you to enhance your self-awareness, which is a critical leadership skill. It is imperative to fully understand yourself, what motivates you, why you act and behave the way you do, and how others perceive or are impacted by you. It also helps you recognize your gifts and strengths, and what opportunities you still develop further. By applying the tools and techniques in this book, you can challenge yourself to move past your fears and learn and grow as a person and leader. To embrace and accept all of you. This transformative journey empowers you to reach your highest potential and to be your best authentic self. That is what the world needs from you now. Step confidently into your light and shine brightly for all to see. You are more powerful than you realize, and stronger than you know. Glow forward with confidence, authenticity, and joy.

# ACKNOWLEDGEMENTS

I have been so blessed on this book writing journey and have so many people to acknowledge for their help and support. First, I want to thank my children Katie and CJ for always being so encouraging and supportive of my taking this challenge on. They have been outstanding teachers for me and I am so blessed to have them in my life. I also want to thank my husband Bob for his patience with me while I toiled at the computer and worked to complete this first book. He has been so accommodating as I moved away from my professional career to begin this new journey as an author and small business owner. I am grateful to my friends and family who helped me to edit and refine my writing. My thanks go to my aunt, Donna Perlee, for her feedback and master's in library science knowledge and skills in editing (and proofreading!) and to my sister, Mary Browne, for her constructive edits and comments.

Kudos to Toi Walker, marketing, and social media guru extraordinaire, and to her team at New Identity Marketing. Not only did they help me craft my brand, but they also have been instrumental in my getting this book and my new business off the ground. My gratitude also goes to Kristy Garay and her company, Exsentos. She has been so helpful with her creative ideas, feedback and encouragement, and her team has supported my Delean Institute for Growth and Wellness business in a variety of ways. Both Kristy and Toi gave me the confidence to complete this book and develop a fun and innovative launch plan. I thank Dr. Macy Punzalan, for her reassuring and caring words of encouragement as I finalized this book. Finally, thank you to Marilyn Liberis for starting me on this journey. You helped me to learn the business of writing and publishing a book and I am eternally indebted to your help. I am also grateful for the team at Balboa Press, who guided me through the self-publishing process.

# SOURCES

## CHAPTER 1

American Merriam Webster Dictionary, www.merriamwebster.com/dictionary/passion

American Merriam Webster Dictionary, www.merriamwebster.com/dictionary/value

Cecchi DiAngelo, Paola, How Self-Awareness Elevates Leadership Effectiveness, February 14, 2024, Forbes, forbes.com

Clear, James, LeaderShape Institute, Core Values List: Over 50 Common Personal Values (jamesclear.com)

Eurich, Tasha, What Self-Awareness Really Is (and how to cultivate it), January 4, 2018, Harvard business Review, hbr.org

Lickerman, Alex, MD, The Undefeated Mind, Psychology Today September 13, 2015, How To Find Your Mission | Psychology Today

Mindtools Content Team, What are Your Values?, What Are Your Values? - Deciding What's Important in Life (mindtools.com)

O'Keefe PA, Dweck CS, Walton GM, Implicit Theory of Interest; _Finding Your Passion or Developing it?,_ Psychol Sci. 2018, 29 (10) 1653-1664.

Rob, Diana, What's Your Passion, June 12, 2017, Psychology Today, pyschologytoday.com

Valterand, Robert, 2008, Harmonious Passion, Psychology Today, psychologytoday.com

Wooll, Maggie, Purpose, Better UP, betterup.com/blog/purpose

## CHAPTER 2

American Merriam Webster Dictionary, www.merriamwebster.com/dictionary/observation

Chopra, Deepak, Levels of Awareness, May 11, 2012, deepakchopra.com

Leonard, Kimberlee, Bottorff, Cassie, What is a Gap Analysis, May 29, 2024, Forbes, forbes.com

## CHAPTER 3

American Society of Quality, _Root Cause Analysis: Simplified Tools and Techniques_ and _Root Cause Analysis: The Core of Problem Solving and Corrective Action_, ASQ Quality Press.

Baumeister, R. F., & Leary, M. R. (1995). The need to belong: Desire for interpersonal attachments as a fundamental human motivation. Psychological Bulletin, 117, 497–529.

Han, Esther, Root Cause Analysis: What it is and How to Perform One, March 7, 2023, Online Harvard Business School

Jung, Carl, Concept of Shadow Self, Shadow Psychology, Better Help, betterhelp.com

Lieberman, Matthew D., *Social: Why our brains are wired to connect.* 2013, Oxford University Press

McLeod, Saul, PhD., Simply Psychology, January 24, 2024, Maslow's Hierarchy of Needs (simplypsychology.org)

Mind Tools Content Team,, 5 Whys - Getting to the Root of a Problem Quickly (mindtools.com)

Perera, Ayes, Self-Actualization in Psychology, January 24, 2024, Simply Psychology, Self-Actualization In Psychology: Theory & Examples (simplypsychology.org), What Is Self-Actualization? Meaning, Theory + Examples (positivepsychology.com),

Toyota, Saakichi, Five Whys Technique, Toyota Industries,1930s

## CHAPTER 4

American Merriam Webster Dictionary, merriamwebster.com/dictionary/expose

Bradford, N, February 5, 2024, Quanta Magazine, What Your Brain Is Doing When You're Not Doing Anything | Quanta Magazine

Brown, Brene, *Daring Greatly,* April 2015, Avery Publishing Group

Brene Brown, *Gifts of Imperfection, Let Go of Who You Think You're Supposed to Be and Embrace Who You Are,* 10th edition, Hazelden, 2010

Christianson, Leah, Kwok, Navio, McShane, Margot, Pye, Hetty, We Should All have Imposter Syndrome, May 20, 2024, Russell Reynolds, russellreynolds.com/en/insights

Chopra, Deepak, *Quantum Body: The New Science for Living a Longer and More Vital Life*, Harmony, New York, 2023

Friedman, Alexandra, Overcoming Imposter Syndrome As an Emerging Leader, Forbes, September 3, 2020, forbes.com/sites/forbescouchcouncil

Hyatt, Michael, Hyatt-Miller, Megan, *Mind Your Mindset The Science That Shows Success Starts with Your Thinking*, Baker Publishing, 2023

## CHAPTER 5

Gotian, Ruth, MD., Overlooked Signs You Are Giving Away Your Power, January 17, 2023, Forbes, <u>Overlooked Signs You Are Giving Away Your Power (forbes.com)</u>,

Melnick, Sharon, PhD.,,*In Your Power, React Less, Regain Control, Raise Others,* 1st Edition, Wiley Publishers, 2022

Rubenstein, Laura, Stepping into Your Power, What Does That Really Mean, October 10, 2023

Van Der Klok, Bessel, *The Body Keeps Score,* Penguin Books, New York, 2015

## CHAPTER 6

American Merriam Webster Dictionary, merriamwebster.com/dictionary/unlock

Associates for Process Improvement

Athey, A., "Stop Playing Small: Embrace Your Inner Power," Psychology Today, December 6, 2021, Stop Playing Small: Embrace Your Inner Power | Psychology Today

Auspicium Neurolinguistic Programming (NLP), NLP Practitioner Certificate Program materials, auspicium.co.uk Cambridge Dictionary,

Cambridge Dictionary, https://dictionary.cambridge.org/dictionary/english/play-small

Collins, Jim, *Good to Great*, 2001, Harper Collins Publishers, 10 E 2nd 53rd Street, New York, New York, pages 164-165.

Demming, W. Edward, Demming Institute, PDSA Cycle - The W. Edwards Deming Institute

Institute for Healthcare Improvement, How to Improve: Model for Improvement | Institute for Healthcare Improvement (ihi.org)

Kay, Katty, Shipman, Claire, "*The Confidence Code*," Harper Business Publishing, 2014.

Mohr, Tara, "*Playing Small, Practical Wisdom for Women Who Want to Speak Up, Create, and Lead*, Penguin Random House, New York, 2015.

Yokes-Dawson Law, 1907, Positive Psychology, positivepsychology.com/toolkit, "Leaving the Comfort Zone"

## CHAPTER 7

Byne, Rhonda, *Secret The Power*, Atria Books, 2010

Berstein, Gabrielle, *Super Attractor, Methods for Manifesting a Life Beyond Your Wildest Dreams*, Hay House, 2019

Hofsted, Six Cultural Dimensions, Masculine vs. Feminine, Simply Psychology, simplypsychology.com

Jain, Jim, How to Adopt a Possibility Mindset, June 23, 2022, Forbes, How To Adopt A Possibility Mindset And Enhance Your Strategy (forbes.com)

O'Connell, Andrews, Sometimes it is Better to Brainstorm Alone, February 4, 2010, Harvard Business Review, hbr.org/2010/0

Paul Plsek, *Directed Creativity, Creativity, Innovation and Quality*, Irwin Professional Publishing, 1997.

Stone Zander, Rosemond, Zander, Ben, *The Art of Possibility, Transforming Personal and Professional Life*, Penguin Books, September 2022

Printed in the United States
by Baker & Taylor Publisher Services